Random House
BACK
TO THE
BEACH
CROSSWORDS

Edited by
Stanley Newman

Random House
Puzzles & Games

_____

SPECIAL SALES

_____

1 ANY WHICH WAY

by Mary E. Brindamour

ACROSS

1 Closed
5 Canonized Mlles.
9 Interrogative pronoun
12 Uses a VCR
14 Lo-cal
15 Camp food
16 Drained of color
17 Emphasize
19 Hedge sculpture
21 "__ With a Kiss"
22 Ease
23 Got a D
24 Tiny critter
26 Author Sinclair
27 Belfry resident
28 Paul of *Crocodile Dundee*
30 __ wave (tsunami)
34 Bit of gossip
36 Factions
38 Caesar's costar
39 Column style
41 Tide types
43 Ironic
44 More cunning
46 Makes amends
48 South Americans
50 Comedian Arnold
51 Convincing
52 Wine mavens
54 Weed-covered
56 Nebraska city
58 Writes
59 Roman poet
60 Hazardous gas
61 Pitcher's stat.
62 Droops
63 Gingrich of Georgia

DOWN

1 RR stop
2 Biblical verb
3 Pad furniture
4 Plains abode
5 Drink noisily
6 Littler than little
7 Airport abbr.
8 Teeter-totter
9 During the time that
10 Sharpened
11 Was in debt
13 Informant
15 Revered work
18 Convene again
20 Sedans
23 Word form for "five"
24 Footnote abbr.
25 Western alliance
26 Shoe sales-man, at times
29 Kelly and Hackman
31 Reduce in importance
32 Land measure
33 Puts down
35 Gentlemen
37 Run-ins
40 Hold on
42 Machine part
45 Prelims
47 Kind of band
48 Sweetheart
49 Booster rocket
50 Smooths
51 Deal (with)
52 Baby branch
53 Put on display
55 Cicero's eggs
57 Picnic pest

2 TRIPLE FEATURE

by Eric Albert

ACROSS

1 Unclear
5 Hot lunch
10 Con game
14 Drama award
15 Great destruction
16 Saint's circle
17 Ignore
20 Barbie's boyfriend
21 *Gentlemen Prefer Blondes* author
22 Small part
23 Actor Arnaz
24 Give a name to
25 Smitten
28 Point of departure
29 Radio regulator: Abbr.
32 Memorable ship
33 Unadulterated
34 2-D extent
35 Scold
38 "If __ I Would Leave You"
39 Of enormous extent
40 Huey, Dewey, and __
41 Writer Deighton
42 Sword handle
43 Like a puppy
44 Ship's tiller
45 Singer Patti
46 Harmony
49 Hunger pain
50 Nightwear
53 Defy
56 Être
57 Obliterate
58 Poet Alexander
59 Out
60 Tools with teeth
61 Once more

DOWN

1 Pawn
2 Ready, willing, and __
3 Jerusalem, figuratively
4 Affirmative answer
5 Opt for
6 Capital of Vietnam
7 Composer Charles
8 __ Alamos, NM
9 Cold drink
10 Unfilled pie
11 Barrel
12 Voice range
13 LEM locale
18 Huddle count
19 New Haven campus
23 Giving person
24 Jeweler's measure
25 Constrain
26 Like a babe in the woods
27 Bedclothes, e.g.
28 Invitee
29 Impostor
30 Beany's buddy
31 Sweet and crumby
33 Sacred song
34 Home
36 Bad guy
37 Nancy's pal
42 Oregano, for one
43 French port
44 Cozy and comfortable
45 Like Nehru jackets
46 "__ girl!"
47 Medium-sized dog
48 Castro's country
49 High point
50 Laborer
51 Wisecrack
52 Fret and fume
54 Gun-lobby grp.
55 Whirlpool bath

3 SHOOTING STARS

by Janie Lyons

ACROSS

1 Freshwater fish
5 Shame
10 Burn slightly
14 Felipe of baseball
15 Italian bowling
16 Nevada city
17 *Butch Cassidy and the Sundance Kid* star
19 Word form for "within"
20 Car-radio feature
21 Captivated
23 Helper: Abbr.
25 Middle
26 Printer's directions
29 Irving or Carter
31 Tips a hat
34 Story
35 Arafat's org.
36 Previously
37 "The Greatest"
38 Helium holder
40 Society column word
41 Poet William
43 Atty.'s degree
44 Pierre's st.
45 Tree bumps
46 Deli bread
47 Hardwood trees
48 __ as a goose
50 Aroma
52 Aetna rival
55 Senator Muskie
59 Harvest
60 *High Noon* star
62 Noun suffix
63 Cop __ (bargain, maybe)
64 Mrs. Nick Charles
65 Danish physicist
66 Oozing
67 Winter forecast

DOWN

1 *Li'l Abner* cartoonist
2 Winglike
3 Don Juan
4 Throb
5 Helps a hood
6 Violinist's need
7 Highest point
8 Meager
9 Siva worshiper
10 __ the crop (finest)
11 *The Tin Star* star
12 Poker stake
13 Crucifix
18 Noted loch
22 German seaport
24 Lofty
26 Pile up
27 Claw
28 *The Magnificent Seven* star
30 Actress Ringwald
32 Anomaly
33 Searches for
35 Golf goal
36 Hope or Newhart
38 Intoxicate
39 Bread spread
42 Flourish
44 Sunday talks
46 Record again
47 Hubbub
49 Adventure stories
51 Corrode
52 Jordanian, for one
53 *Tonight Show* host
54 __ Stanley Gardner
56 Well-informed
57 Pianist Peter
58 Sketch
61 Slangy assent

4 MATTERS OF TASTE

by Dean Niles

ACROSS

1 Dull
5 Bogged down
10 "Waterloo" group
14 Leak slowly
15 Rub out
16 Wedding-cake level
17 Disdain for the unobtainable
19 List entry
20 EMT procedure
21 Gave temporarily
22 Insignificant
24 Serengeti sillies?
26 Please, in Potsdam
27 Serious cinema
30 Gun an engine
33 It makes waste
36 *Picnic* playwright
37 Brooks and Gibson
38 Part of QED
39 Burn
40 Yardstick org.
41 Comrade
42 Tom Joad, for one
43 Appendix neighbor
44 Little child
45 Deviating
47 Aviator Post
49 Calf
53 More economical
55 Headliner
57 1300 hours
58 Courtly instrument
59 Widespread craving
62 Sign of the future
63 Rockies range
64 Floundering
65 Peel an orange
66 Roman parent
67 Balkan

DOWN

1 Painter Hieronymus
2 Daft
3 Blue hue
4 __ *Alibi* ('89 movie)
5 Slightest
6 Isfahan's country
7 Engrossed
8 Journal ending
9 Very unpopular
10 Leaning
11 Furthest extremity
12 Bar order
13 Troops
18 Annoying light
23 Dined
25 Cooper hero Bumppo
26 Morning musician
28 *The Iceman Cometh* character
29 Studio sign
31 Otherwise
32 Engine option
33 Solar output
34 Singer Guthrie
35 Taffy type
37 Devilfish
39 Regains control
43 Motionless
45 Bristol brew
46 Personification
48 Actress Worth
50 On the prowl
51 Computer key
52 Fix up
53 Hog food
54 Mountain lion
55 Transmitted
56 Head: Fr.
60 Mil. stat.
61 US alliance

5 COUPLES

by Shirley Soloway

ACROSS

1 Birthday figures
5 Talks wildly
10 "__ boy!"
14 Burrowing rodent
15 Similar
16 Clean the deck
17 Poker hand
19 Become winded
20 Step
21 Hummingbird's home
22 Picnic pests
23 Out of kilter
25 Spew forth
27 Serves the soup
30 __ David (religious symbol)
32 Greek love god
33 Border on
36 Whines
38 R-V center
39 Car coloration
41 Shoe width
42 Rome's river
44 Neck part
45 Soho streetcar
46 Screenwriter May
48 '92 Wimbledon winner
50 Therefore
51 Hunt or Hayes
53 Env. notation
55 Designer Cassini
57 Carpenter's items
61 French silk
62 Simon and Garfunkel, e.g.
64 Diminutive dogs
65 "Untouchable" Ness
66 *Desire Under the __*
67 Editor's word
68 Office worker
69 Taken-back auto

DOWN

1 Electrical units
2 Capricorn symbol
3 Director Kazan
4 Ongoing dramas
5 Brit. fliers
6 Thicke and Young
7 Bad habits
8 Gets by, with "out"
9 Six-line verse
10 Rogers' partner
11 Kuala Lumpur skyscraper pair
12 Fruit pastry
13 Vigoda and Burrows
18 *Coffee, Tea, __?*
24 "__ Mommy Kissing Santa Claus"
26 Fictional aunt
27 For fear that
28 Bandleader Shaw
29 Holiday pay rate
30 Corner sign
31 Dog lovers?
34 Skeleton part
35 Actress Hagen
37 Big rig
39 Math subject
40 Actress Patricia
43 Purposeful
45 Scarlet bird
47 Rope loops
49 British actor Leo
51 Skater Sonja
52 Encourage vigorously
53 Vipers
54 Horn-blower's sound
56 Cheerful song
58 Run in neutral
59 Sugar serving
60 Mediocre
63 "How was __ know?"

6 COURSE WORK

by Nancy Salomon

ACROSS

1 Toe woe
5 Fundamental
10 Duel tool
14 Peek-__
15 Luncheonette lure
16 Pop
17 Pest-control devices
19 Tend the sauce
20 Shortstop Reese
21 Back-pedals
23 *Born Free* lioness
25 Tilted
26 Roman garments
29 Faux __
31 Disdain
34 Ache
35 Buck and bull
36 Coins
37 Chowed down
38 Terrestrial
40 "In what way?"
41 Lofty goals
43 Rogers or Clark
44 Cherry stones
45 Tunes
46 Hilarious Hope
47 Slightly stewed
48 Nimble
50 Just for the fun __
52 Add to
55 Summaries
59 Wear out
60 Battle of 1775
62 Dollar bills
63 Do-__ situation (crisis)
64 Buffalo waterfront
65 Famed loch
66 Musical pauses
67 Turned blue?

DOWN

1 Summer place
2 Woodwind
3 Libertine
4 "Piece of cake!"
5 Last name in motels?
6 Part of ETA
7 Fly high
8 Forces
9 Social class
10 Lifeblood
11 TV snack
12 Prepare for publication
13 Head set?
18 Slippery swimmers
22 Grating
24 Copycat
26 Bangkok natives
27 Exceed
28 Gabor sitcom
30 Houston ballplayer
32 Uproars
33 Full of the latest
35 Owns
36 Like a fox
38 Beast of Borden
39 Freight-car hopper
42 Start a fight
44 Threw a strike
46 "How Can I __?" ('67 tune)
47 Row
49 Sweat and slave
51 Releases
52 Pour __ (strive)
53 Workday start
54 Pass catchers
56 Well-ventilated
57 Ballet bend
58 Toboggan
61 Hobby-shop buy

7 WHAT'S COOKING?

by Shirley Soloway

ACROSS

1 "Too bad!"
5 *Butterfield 8* author
10 Freshwater fish
14 Marquis de __
15 Boca __, FL
16 Mata __
17 Become calm
19 Gymnast Korbut
20 "For want of __ . . ."
21 Mornings: Abbr.
22 High-pitched flutes
23 Mouth pros
25 Restrain
26 Have a bite
27 Prohibited
30 Pinky or Peggy
33 "My lips are __"
36 Creole veggie
37 Shade trees
39 Make corrections
40 Century segment
41 Singer Lane
42 Waistline
44 Two-bagger: Abbr.
45 Marched up Main
47 Wynn and Asner
49 Had a mortgage
50 Kept harassing
55 Court session
57 A long way off
58 __ Gay

59 Shopping center
60 Lost one's temper
62 Daredevil Knievel
63 Tears down
64 Geom. shape
65 Sparks and Beatty
66 Prayer endings
67 Sciences' partner

DOWN

1 Syrian leader
2 Singer Frankie
3 Jingle guy
4 Hebrew, e.g.
5 Hockey great Bobby
6 Attacked
7 Particles
8 Moves a canoe
9 Actress Jillian
10 Church vocalist
11 Poorly planned
12 Give encouragement
13 Diagonal
18 Inventor Howe
22 Mink or beaver
24 Irritated
25 Fussed over
27 Ward (off)
28 Dreary
29 British nobleman
30 Spring
31 Exile isle
32 In a state of confusion

34 In the thick of
35 Went first
38 Beach barriers
43 Sidled
46 Dover's home: Abbr.
48 Hacienda housewife
50 Pool-table fabric
51 Songwriter Harold
52 Fido's friend
53 Put in office
54 Pub game
55 Nitti nabbers
56 Boffo review
57 Shaving cream
60 Swimsuit top
61 Road curve

NUMBERS GAME

by Harvey Estes

ACROSS

1 Basics
5 Word used in dating
10 Spoken
14 Former Senate leader
15 Intense hatred
16 Red in the middle
17 Slot machines
20 Youth org.
21 Bunch together
22 Light brown
23 Range of hearing
25 Gum ingredient
28 "Absolutely!" in Baja
29 "O'er" opposite
32 Cranny companion
33 Fleur-de-__
35 Oz coward
37 Hot-shot pilot
38 Opinion
42 Wrath
43 With respect to
44 Matter for future generations?
45 Noun suffix
47 Noncom, for short
49 Row
53 Soup pot
55 Mickey's Florida home
57 Before, in verse
58 Put a match to
60 Ran for cover
61 Picnic contest
65 Scottish isle
66 Name on a plane
67 Choir member
68 Classroom furniture

69 Inserted a gusset
70 Army eatery

DOWN

1 Desert bricks
2 Teensy tree
3 Frees from blame
4 Neptune's domain
5 Practical smarts
6 Have a notion
7 Gets free (of)
8 Baby bears
9 GP grp.
10 Install a minister
11 April apparel
12 Carney or Linkletter

13 __ Misérables
18 Stadium shout
19 To the __ degree
24 Farm building
25 Dunce
26 __ Lomond
27 Just manage, with "out"
30 Change
31 "__ the season . . ."
34 Here, in Le Havre
36 Persona __ grata
38 Family framework
39 Zane Grey works
40 New Deal org.

41 Pro __ (proportionately)
42 Squid's squirt
46 Silver __ ('76 film)
48 Stare at
50 Take a breath
51 Royal decrees
52 Cowboy competitions
54 Martial arts master
56 Inc., in England
58 Late-night name
59 Frankenstein's assistant
61 Dosage schedule: Abbr.
62 Weeding tool
63 Chicken piece
64 Zodiac symbol

9 FAMILIAR TRIO

by Dean Niles

ACROSS

1 Mike problem
5 Stoneworker
10 Not quite closed
14 Failure
15 Low joint
16 Hold sway
17 Prerecord
18 Nasty
19 Some agents
20 C-__ (cable channel)
21 Drill sergeant's shout
22 __ down (shut up)
23 Be
25 Showy shrub
28 Copied perfectly
30 Richard of *Pretty Woman*
31 Sugar qty.
34 Cowboy country
35 Hostess Perle
36 Tango quorum
37 Omelet ingredients
38 Emcee Hall
39 "__ a Lady" ('71 tune)
40 Wine word
41 __ Island (Brooklyn resort area)
42 Touches
43 Choral syllable
44 Gardener, at times
45 Forecaster
46 Sonoran snooze
48 One of the musical B's
49 Sun screen
51 __ Mahal
53 Reagan Cabinet member
56 Go over a manuscript
57 France's longest river
59 Professor 'iggins
60 Helen's mother
61 Impassive
62 Read quickly
63 __ of Our Lives
64 Mr. Chips portrayer
65 Camper's shelter

DOWN

1 Salamanders
2 Show approval
3 Early TV cowboy
4 Job slots
5 Prepared potatoes
6 Singer Murray
7 Some traits do this
8 __ Maid (card game)
9 Society-page word
10 Bandleader Shaw
11 Consent avidly
12 On the sheltered side
13 Pull apart
22 Urgent appeal
24 Kind of neckline
26 Full of pep
27 Pretentious
28 Wave top
29 Bar order
32 Bulge
33 Sheriff's band
35 French Impressionist
38 Cattle calls
39 Naval footlocker
41 *Silkwood* star
42 __ Angelico
45 Beg to differ
47 Tiny bits
49 Prairie, in Pretoria
50 Notion
52 *Aida* selection
54 Tehran's country
55 Peer __
57 Psychedelic letters
58 Word form for "ear"

ACROSS

1 Star in Orion
6 Squint (at)
10 *Sesame Street* subject
14 Love a lot
15 Gen. Robt. __
16 Heap
17 Chopin's favorite novelist
19 Ken of *thirtysomething*
20 Weaken
21 It's a small matter
22 Voting sheet
24 School grps.
25 With merriment
26 Labor leader Gompers
29 Stout spots
32 Dumbstruck
33 Metric weights
34 Dovecote sound
35 Pisa dough
36 __ the Barbarian
37 Blackbird
38 Caribou kin
39 Jeans alternative
40 Put a halt to
41 French ladies
43 Cautioned
44 Florida city
45 Chaplin prop
46 Eye part
48 *Casablanca* role
49 Brown shade
52 *Diary of __ Housewife*
53 Smooch-throwing TV hostess
56 Jennifer on *WKRP*
57 "Oh, fiddle-faddle!"
58 Bulova rival
59 Pie á la __
60 Baseballer Cabell
61 Alamogordo event

DOWN

1 Old clothes
2 Birth of a notion?
3 Sticky stuff
4 Foul up
5 Heir
6 Chihuahua cash
7 Western star Jack
8 Sundown, to Shelley
9 Snoopy's foe
10 Artemis' twin
11 "Caribbean Queen" singer
12 Advertising award
13 Faxed or telexed
18 List ender
23 Superciliousness
24 Insect stage
25 Big bashes
26 Hawthorne's hometown
27 Well-coordinated
28 Former US poet laureate
29 Ties up
30 Code name?
31 Did some cobbling
33 Seoul site
36 Buddy
37 Only
39 Showed up
40 Rummy variety
42 __ Dinmont terrier
43 Do the laundry
45 Social stratum
46 Self-possessed
47 *Typee* sequel
48 Fascinated by
49 Big book
50 Bellicose deity
51 Waiting-room cry
54 Scottish John
55 Song that sells

11 MOVIE MARATHON

by Shirley Soloway

ACROSS

1 Adam of *Batman*
5 Prepares to shoot
9 Mr. Brinker
13 Psychedelic musical
14 Legal paper
15 Repetitive behavior
16 Land measure
17 Top-quality
18 Actress Verdugo
19 '86 Fonda film
22 Sugary suffix
23 Tach meas.
24 Intelligent
27 Fluffy neckpiece
29 Tobacco dryer
33 Charged particle
34 Menace
37 __ consequence (unimportant)
38 '75 Pacino film
41 Popular cookie
42 Idle
43 Mine find
44 Actress Carter
45 Cat or canary
46 Politician picker
48 Greek consonant
50 Mongrel
51 '50 Widmark film
60 Warbucks' waif
61 Diva's performance
62 Israeli dance
63 Daring act
64 Tailor's tools
65 Participating
66 The biggest Cartwright
67 Fencing weapon
68 Unpleasantly damp

DOWN

1 Start of a query
2 Apiece
3 Kingly address
4 Aftershock
5 Having knowledge (of)
6 Heavy metal
7 Short skirt
8 British gun
9 Heavenly sight
10 Help a hood
11 Baseball team
12 Head the cast
15 Pile high
20 Caesar's port
21 School records
24 Lebanese city
25 Actress Demi
26 Jockey Cordero
27 Suit
28 In the know
30 In progress
31 Nap noisily
32 Copier need
35 Nearsightedness
36 Fancy appetizer
39 Marineland attractions
40 Variety show
47 Tropical flower
49 Printer's notation
50 Go after
51 Poet Ogden
52 Division word
53 Wildebeests
54 Back of the neck
55 Faucet fault
56 Fork point
57 New Rochelle college
58 '82 Jeff Bridges film
59 Pull sharply

by Bob Lubbers

ACROSS

1 Ameche role
5 Socialist Eugene
9 Actor Buddy
14 Bread spread
15 Dynamic start
16 Bingo alternative
17 Foothold
19 Navigation system
20 One after another
21 Cover story?
23 Inlets
26 "I Let __ Go Out Of My Heart" ('38 tune)
28 Make Mickey move
31 __ Howser, M.D.
33 Sikorsky and Stravinsky
34 Devoured
36 Prohibit
37 Sunburn soother
38 Fills to the gills
39 Deflect, with "off"
40 Actor Beatty
41 Send payment
42 Mild oaths
43 Seasoned
45 Ideas
47 French river
48 Pesky insect
49 Drink noisily
51 Maximum
56 Sand bar
58 Former Texas arena
61 Dracula's title
62 __ En-lai
63 Bumbler
64 "High __" ('59 song)
65 Spud buds
66 Falls behind

DOWN

1 Boyish cuts
2 "Waiting for the Robert __"
3 Producer Norman
4 Places
5 Showy flower
6 Foot width
7 Lingerie item
8 Bar supply
9 Sci-fi writer Harlan
10 Small error
11 Skinny veggie
12 Airport abbr.
13 __ sequitur
18 Injures
22 Fills the hold
24 Hannibal Smith and company
25 Usher's activity
27 Jets' rivals
28 Shining brightly
29 Lunch favorite
30 Fury
32 Extremities
33 Fleming and McShane
35 Rockies range
38 Exodus commemoration
39 To and __
41 Final tallies
42 "Same here!"
44 New Orleans campus
46 Zodiac sign
50 Gallop or trot
52 1650, to Tiberius
53 Oop's girlfriend
54 Polluted air
55 Knight and Turner
56 Tchrs.' workplace
57 Owl's cry
59 Bashful
60 Sock part

13 ALL SMILES

by Shirley Soloway

ACROSS

1 Notice
5 "I've Got __ in Kalamazoo"
9 Taj Mahal town
13 Siamese
14 Flag holders
16 Israeli airline
17 Birth, e.g.
19 Author Sheehy
20 Pencil end
21 In an impassive way
23 Aspin or Paul
24 __ standstill
26 Whiskey type
27 Gumdrop brand
29 __ rule (usually)
32 Rampur royalty
35 __ Tin Tin
36 Daisy Mae's man
38 "__ Rhythm"
39 Revises a text
42 Inactive
43 Assertion
45 Service charge
46 College degs.
47 Make a mistake
48 Choral group
52 Thoughts
54 Ocean vessel: Abbr.
55 Mythical bird
58 Auto-racer Mario
61 Performer Pia
63 Scott of *Charles in Charge*
64 Loud guffaw
66 Stopping places
67 One who watches
68 Mr. Laurel
69 One-liners
70 Transatlantic planes
71 Coop critters

DOWN

1 Lucy's landlady
2 Be generous
3 The Mamas and the __
4 Puppy sounds
5 Opening
6 State VIP
7 Bristol brews
8 Soup ingredient
9 Sponsorship
10 Seeks votes
11 Support on the stairs
12 Comrade-in-arms
15 Pack away
18 Slangy assent
22 Hartman or Bonet
25 Battery contents
27 Feline musical
28 Butter spreader
30 Ward of *Sisters*
31 Greek war god
32 Come up in the world
33 Thickening agent
34 Teenage pastime
37 Lettuce choice
40 Gumshoes
41 Carbonated drinks
44 Architectural detail
49 Wood strips
50 Bars legally
51 Russian range
53 Metal waste
55 Highway
56 Church instrument
57 Lyricist Sammy et al.
58 __ *Hand for the Little Lady*
59 *Peter Pan* pooch
60 Eye part
62 Short race
65 Congeal

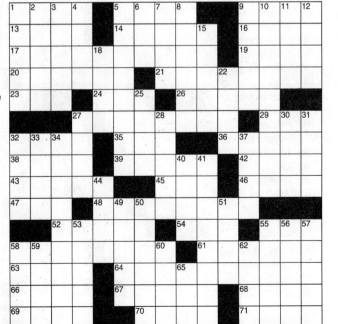

by Dean Niles

ACROSS

1 Pizazz
6 Trombone accessory
10 For fear that
14 Light weight
15 In __ (stuck)
16 Curtain-raiser
17 Seuss tale
20 Put in stitches
21 Dehydrates
22 Solo
23 Photog.'s item
24 Behind schedule
26 Dervish
29 Plain to see
31 __ kwon do
34 Healing plant
35 In accord
36 Verbal noun
38 Anthony Burgess book, with *A*
41 Offer shelter to
42 Collection
43 Harness part
44 Timid
45 Cantaloupe or casaba
47 Ancient Persians
48 Soft drink
49 Melody
50 Oriental
53 *Jaws* menace
56 Soft touch
59 '68 Beatles movie
62 First name in daredeviltry
63 Sign on
64 *Divine Comedy* poet
65 Alluring
66 Holler
67 Furry fish-eater

DOWN

1 Beclouds
2 Entice
3 Once again
4 The __ Capades
5 Hand over
6 Biblical trio
7 Coax
8 Scuffle vigorously
9 Frat letter
10 Serve the minestrone
11 Reverberation
12 Ollie's other half
13 Use a stopwatch
18 Work unit
19 Talk and talk
23 Family member
25 Tech talk
26 The truth
27 God of Islam
28 Eccentric
29 Lennon's lady
30 Left-hand page
31 Brought into pitch
32 Actress Dickinson
33 Happy places
35 Possessed
37 Less available
39 Kurosawa costume
40 Barbie's beau
46 Timmy's pet
47 G&S character
48 "Long Tall __" ('56 tune)
49 Supply with weapons
50 Some votes
51 Golfer Ballesteros
52 Holly shrub
54 Throw forcefully
55 Cain's victim
56 Add some color
57 Poker stake
58 Jury member
60 Youngster's query
61 Inform (on)

15 IN HIS POCKET

by Mary Brindamour

ACROSS

1 Movie terrier
5 Guru
10 Not quite closed
14 Sudden idea
15 __ of Troy
16 Colorless
17 Elastic device
19 Computer symbol
20 Pub potable
21 Sneezer's need
22 Got by, with "out"
23 WWII general
25 Peanuts or popcorn
27 Signed an agreement
30 Prevailing tendencies
33 French Impressionist
36 Light beer
38 Debtor's letters
39 Greek love god
40 Philanthropist
41 Canadian prov.
42 Building wing
43 Polite refusal
44 Borscht ingredient
45 Braves the bully
47 Electrical inventor
49 Orchestra section
51 Compassionate ones
55 Jai __
57 NHL player
60 Mauna __
61 Officeholders

62 Staples alternatives
64 Ready, willing, and __
65 Crème de la crème
66 March 15th, e.g.
67 Mrs. Dick Tracy
68 Derby and dash
69 Extremely

DOWN

1 "That's __!" ("All done!")
2 Miami coach Don
3 Lama land
4 Diplomatic off.
5 Grow smaller
6 Spider's snares
7 "Woe is me!"

8 Waiter's handouts
9 Typesetter, at times
10 For each
11 Whittling tool
12 Lotion additive
13 Tear apart
18 Short jackets
24 Acapulco aunts
26 O'Hare abbr.
28 Yale students
29 Ship's crane
31 Blockhead
32 Soapy water
33 Feat
34 __ Stanley Gardner
35 Tee toppers
37 Richard of Pretty Woman

40 Blabbermouth
41 At hand
43 Teachers' org.
44 Mont __ (French peak)
46 Eye parts
48 Intimidates
50 La __ Opera House
52 Skip over
53 Cowboy, at times
54 Impertinent
55 Get __ on the back
56 Earring locale
58 The Aeneid, for one
59 Apportion, with "out"
63 Actress Ullmann

16 ASTRONOMICAL

by Fred Piscop

ACROSS
1 Stowe sight
6 Boxcar rider
10 Shed
14 Quinn of *Reckless*
15 Daredevil Knievel
16 Butter substitute
17 Ecumenical Council site
18 "__ 'em and weep!"
19 Gulf state
20 Birds' prey
22 __ Scotia
23 Coffeemaker
24 Mortarboard ornament
26 Bold
30 Sportscaster Musburger
32 Singer Lenya
33 Tater topper
37 Tony Musante series
38 Whipped-cream servings
39 Forearm bone
40 Put in the autoclave
42 Offspring
43 Foul liquid
44 Turnstile fodder
45 Drives back
48 Moray
49 Fitzgerald of jazz
50 Shades
57 Carson predecessor
58 On the briny
59 Adorable one

60 Ear-related
61 __ *Poets Society*
62 Major happening
63 Clockmaker Thomas
64 Goofs up
65 Coolidge's veep

DOWN
1 Stuff to the gills
2 Cremona cash
3 European river
4 Huff and puff
5 Bubble over
6 Wading bird
7 Above
8 "__ me up, Scotty!"

9 Seniors
10 '87 Cher film
11 Actor Edward James __
12 Corporal's time off
13 Having musical qualities
21 Twisted
25 Mandela's grp.
26 Diner orders
27 Plant part
28 "Ma! (He's Making Eyes __)"
29 Ed McMahon show
30 Hooch
31 Cartoonist Goldberg

33 Slender
34 Nobelist Wiesel
35 Shortly
36 Picks a crew
38 Ballet slide
41 "Well, __ be!"
42 Consoled
44 __ Aviv
45 Seized autos
46 Thrill
47 *S'il vous __*
48 "Zounds!"
51 __-friendly
52 Around the corner
53 Fiji's capital
54 Fret
55 "__ *kleine Nachtmusik*"
56 Collections

17 CARTOON COUPLES

by Fred Piscop

ACROSS

1 Shortstop Pee Wee
6 Iowa city
10 Comic Sahl
14 Magna __
15 Church section
16 Region
17 Specialized lingo
18 Genealogy diagram
19 *Jurassic Park* beast, for short
20 Cartoon couple
23 Wave top
24 Slugger Ralph
25 Confront boldly
28 To __ (without exception)
30 Ice-cream flavor: Abbr.
31 Lively dance
33 Climbing plant
36 Cartoon couple
40 Ecology org.
41 Hostess Perle
42 Western sch.
43 Window frame
44 Actress Rolle
46 Valuable violin
49 More sensible
51 Cartoon couple
56 Fall
57 __ *Three Lives*
58 Taxi device
60 Fill with cargo
61 Give a hoot
62 Bring together
63 *For Your __ Only*
64 Famous pirate
65 Landing area

DOWN

1 Communications co.
2 Lawman Wyatt
3 As a result
4 Hand-operated valve
5 Diner patrons
6 Feeds the kitty
7 French Revolution name
8 Level
9 Bird food
10 Actress Marlee
11 Senator Hatch
12 Superman portrayer
13 Congress, e.g.
21 "Are we there __?"
22 Giraffe relative
25 Pinnacle
26 Cookie nugget
27 Caesar's partner
28 *M*A*S*H* star
29 Family member
31 Nasty cut
32 Aardvark morsel
33 Ruler marking
34 Disgusting
35 Fiscal span
37 High-tech memo
38 __-man (toady)
39 Vitamin or mineral
43 Ear bone
44 Conclusion
45 Irish poet Heaney
46 Confuse
47 Tropical eel
48 Battery terminal
49 Memorable Mortimer
50 Threw in
52 Clark or Cavett
53 Jai __
54 Recipe instruction
55 Himalayan legend
59 Agent, for short

18 ROUND AND ROUND

by Shirley Soloway

ACROSS

1 Heated tubs
5 Knightly titles
9 Lassoed
14 Verb tense
15 Take a tumble
16 La Scala performance
17 Tennis great Arthur
18 Barrett or Jaffe
19 Significant others
20 Negotiate
23 Breadthless?
24 Big rig
25 Hit the slopes
28 Dos Passos trilogy
30 Harness up
32 Wide awake
36 Middle weight?
39 Ward of *Sisters*
40 Pulls apart
41 Take __ (snooze)
42 Maytag function
44 Spiner of *Star Trek: The Next Generation*
45 Gets up
46 Cardiologists' org.
48 Vane dir.
49 Paint layer
52 African antelopes
57 Ideal perspective
59 Go to pot
62 Prego rival
63 Antitoxins
64 Foot bones
65 Desire deified
66 Touch up articles
67 Confused
68 "¿Cómo __ usted?"
69 Actress Daly

DOWN

1 Generate
2 Turkish title
3 *My Name Is __ Lev*
4 Take the reins
5 Soda sippers
6 Golf club
7 Lemon peels
8 Detective Sam
9 Lettuce variety
10 Iridescent birthstone
11 Favorite
12 Prior to, in poetry
13 Trial VIPs
21 Oaf
22 Mideast rulers
25 Book part
26 Designer Donna
27 Maladroit
29 "Just __!" ("Hold on!")
31 Play the lead
32 City on the Nile
33 Absorb
34 Borden bovine
35 Cheerleader shouts
37 Good buddy
38 Vicinity
40 Emmy-winner Cicely
43 Patron saint of music
44 Cotton bundle
47 Mythical menace
50 Go along (with)
51 Peter and Alexander
53 Valuable property
54 Wanting
55 "Mack the Knife" singer
56 Give an opinion
57 Upswing
58 "__ Rhythm"
59 RR depot
60 Bit of butter
61 Hosp. areas

19 LEND A HAND

by Trip Payne

ACROSS

1 Nile slitherers
5 Lease charge
9 Razor sharpener
14 Actor's goal
15 Singer Adams
16 Billy Joel's instrument
17 Astronaut Shepard
18 Impressionist Carvey
19 Drive forward
20 *Cheers* nickname
23 Finish the cupcakes
24 Victory symbol
25 Snuggle
29 Suit fabric
31 Identical
34 Wreak havoc on
35 Work unit
37 *Reine*'s husband
38 Woodwind instrument
39 Schoolyard retort
43 *Elephant Boy* actor
44 Baden-Baden, for one
45 Mauna __
46 Related
47 Foots the bill
49 "I give up!"
53 Tease a bit
55 Silly Putty container
57 Swiss river
58 '65 Beach Boys tune
62 Comic Myron
65 Corporate symbol
66 Writing tablets
67 Expect
68 All over again
69 Fencer's choice
70 Italian sauce
71 Ripped
72 Unpopular kid

DOWN

1 A Musketeer
2 Comfort
3 Team member
4 Put in the mail
5 Change colors again
6 *Daniel Boone* actor
7 1492 vessel
8 Greenish blue
9 Backbone
10 This typeface
11 Knock sharply
12 *A Chorus Line* number
13 Campaigner, for short
21 Olympics official Brundage
22 *Anna Christie* playwright
26 "Oom-pah" instrument
27 Jungle king
28 Chemical suffix
30 Post-sneeze remark
32 Deck out
33 Cry from the pasture
36 Mahalia's music
39 Rice wine
40 Drama award
41 "__ Lazy River"
42 Moolah
43 __ Luis Obispo, CA
48 Folk singer Pete
50 Party snack
51 Roofer's need
52 Rubbed out
54 Slowly, to Solti
56 No longer a child
59 Land map
60 Uni- relative
61 Unlocked
62 Mortarboard
63 Must pay
64 Possesses

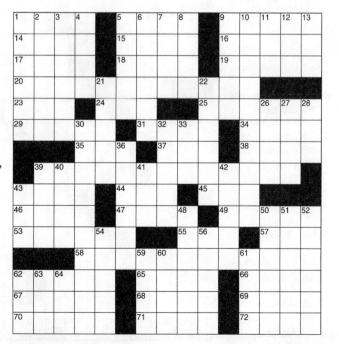

20 SLOW DOWN

by Dean Niles

ACROSS

1 Sot's sound
7 Dog doc
10 Baltimore player
11 Main character
12 Comic Conway
15 Seeing someone
16 Part of A.D.
17 Record label
18 __ *Man Answers* ('62 film)
19 Corporate raider's payoff
21 Timber tool
23 Lions' pride
24 First name in daredeviltry
25 Hamelin hero
27 Go-getters
28 Dad's lad
29 Wordsworth works
30 Coyote cry
31 Pulver's rank: Abbr.
32 Green garnish
34 List abbr.
37 African snakes
39 Steak state
40 Greek letter
41 Whoop it up
43 Tough and shrewd
45 Mesopotamian deity
46 Chelsea's former cat
47 Coll. sports org.
48 French Canadian
50 Hardwood
51 Network in *Network*

52 Mountain pool
53 Where to spend a drachma
56 Scarf down
57 Rugged rock
58 *Seinfeld*, for one
59 "Hold it!"
60 "A-Tisket A-__"

DOWN

1 Coal scuttle
2 One of the Gershwins
3 Legal recourse
4 Arranged a do
5 Arm bone
6 Wooden pin
7 Thin coating

8 Sea birds
9 Fudd, for one
11 Track activity
12 Vacation convenience
13 Less friendly
14 Shopping places
19 Staring one
20 Kitty's comment
21 Church recess
22 The Belmonts' leader
23 He had the touch
26 Seed source
27 Senior member
30 Cattle groups

33 Carefree excursions
35 __ *Team* (Mr. T series)
36 Musical conclusion
38 Wild guess
41 Irritate
42 Caribbean island
43 Cry of joy
44 Beginnings
46 Frighten
49 Engrave a design
50 Opera offering
53 Canadian levy: Abbr.
54 Runner Sebastian
55 CPR expert

21 NEATLY DONE

by Randolph Ross

ACROSS

1 __ seed (deteriorate)
5 __ & Moe (Gleason film)
9 Give forth
13 Actor Mischa
14 __ Now (Murrow TV show)
16 Congenial
17 Stain remover
19 Aware of
20 Throw forcefully
21 Abates
23 Cause a riot
26 Values
27 Late, in La Paz
28 Part of SBLI
29 Licentious
31 Andy's friend
32 Mornings: Abbr.
33 Cash in
35 Sass
36 Has hopes
38 Inventor Whitney
39 Next to hit
41 Family member
42 Peak
43 Spiritual leader
44 Fast plane
45 Seven, in Seville
46 Junior's custodian
48 Repaired a road
49 Parlor furniture
51 Feels off
52 "__ the Rainbow"
53 Tanners
58 Swampland
59 Roman river
60 Sweet sandwich

61 Actress Lanchester
62 "So long!"
63 Like some buildup

DOWN

1 Wander (about)
2 __ Town (Wilder play)
3 Mystery writer Josephine
4 Prom flowers
5 Grenoble's river
6 Enthusiasm
7 Eastern discipline
8 Gives way
9 Shipwrecked, perhaps

10 Naval vessel
11 Religious symbol
12 Perfect scores, at times
15 Oak or elm
18 Early guitar
22 Silly Soupy
23 Author Calvino
24 Identifying
25 Rural aircraft
26 Knowledgeable one
28 Troublesome tyke
30 Strike out
32 Invite
33 Buttons or Barber
34 Made cocktails
36 Sharp

37 Snitch
40 African country
42 Aviation display
44 Georgetown educator
45 Common seasoning
47 Try out
48 Ornate headwear
49 "__ Enchanted Evening"
50 Satanic
51 Cooperate with criminals
54 Jordan's org.
55 Southpaw stat.
56 Reviewer Reed
57 Oriental sauce

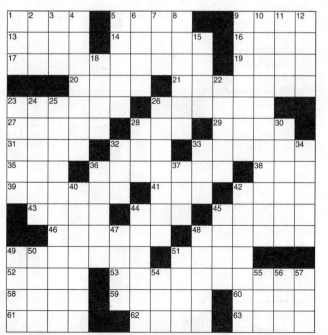

ACROSS

1 To be: Lat.
5 Nest egg, for short
8 Mensa stats
11 Pesky bug
13 Southwestern sight
15 Slashes the budget
17 Managed to include
19 Employ
20 Bilko and Kovacs
21 Wilander of tennis
23 Zuider __
24 Emulate Cicero
26 Little troublemakers
28 Jumping-peg game
31 Old Testament book
32 Eastern discipline
33 Burden
35 Plops down
37 Chores
40 Warm up the oven
42 Love the attention
44 __ up (evaluates)
45 Cable channel
47 Pianist Peter
48 Approximately
50 Medical suffix
52 Tell (on)
53 '87 Danny DeVito film
55 More adventurous
57 Eyebrow shape

58 Con
60 Saudi __
64 Short play
66 Evening out
68 Falls below the horizon
69 Family member
70 Compel
71 Hair coloring
72 Summer quencher
73 Dietitians' amts.

DOWN

1 Facility
2 Roman initials
3 Cold-shoulder
4 Rural refrain?
5 __ Mine (George Harrison book)
6 Beef or lamb

7 It's east of the Urals
8 I, in Innsbruck
9 Game-show host
10 Throat germ
12 Tractor name
14 On edge
16 Understands
18 Eva's sister
22 *Ivanhoe* man
25 Hackneyed
27 Another time
28 Beer ingredient
29 Calvary inscription
30 Former Philippine capital
34 Colonel Potter, to friends
36 They may be deviated

38 Turkish river
39 Primer pooch
41 Road curves
43 Beast
46 Doctor Freud
49 "Christmas comes but __ year . . ."
51 Letter stroke
53 Russian news agency
54 Annoyed
56 Stubble scraper
59 Blue hue
61 Finch, e.g.
62 Peruvian Indian
63 "Rock of __"
65 Poetic monogram
67 Devoured

23 VOCALIZING

by Fred Piscop

ACROSS

1. US Airways competitor
4. Catlike animal
9. *M*A*S*H* character
14. Mil. unit
15. Not so congenial
16. Make reparation
17. Get mellower
18. Newscast image
20. Get together
22. Revives
23. Kett of the comics
24. *Sophie's Choice* author
26. Bumpkin
29. Fix a flat
33. Clothing
36. Arafat's grp.
38. __ Claire, WI
39. Musical message
43. Hosp. area
44. "Inka Dinka __"
45. Saps
46. __ *Is Born*
49. Tugboat or gravy boat
51. Least suntanned
53. Anthem starter
57. Unwelcome guest
60. Chosen child
63. Dental deadener
65. Supply with weapons
66. Roast host
67. Some tournaments
68. Compete
69. Willing one
70. Bronco show
71. Evening, in poetry

DOWN

1. Identify a caller
2. "Ain't __ Fun?"
3. 007, e.g.
4. Give as an example
5. "Not if __ help it!"
6. Most disgusting
7. "A mouse!"
8. Tot's transport
9. Ames Brothers tune of '50
10. Daughter of Zeus
11. "Easy __ it!"
12. Med. student's course
13. Make over
19. Neither's partner
21. Flier to Rio
25. Treads softly
27. Geller the spoonbender
28. Transmit
30. Actress Garr
31. James of *Brian's Song*
32. Sings with closed lips
33. India's continent
34. Spasms
35. Hardware item
37. Early automaker
40. State's head
41. "... __ I saw Elba"
42. Lively dance
47. Orbit point
48. Bacon serving
50. Put on a play
52. Hawaiian souvenir
54. Barrel part
55. Raptor's nest
56. Mideast land
57. "__ a Song Go . . ."
58. Cass, for one
59. Hockey need
61. "Great" dog
62. __ buco
64. Main mail place: Abbr.

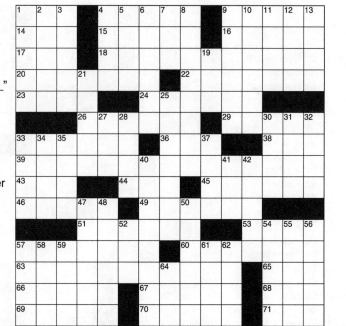

ACROSS
1 Uncooked
4 *Little Women* character
8 Stands behind
13 Western actor Jack
15 Fencing weapon
16 Lofty spaces
17 Top-notch
18 Pharmacy bottle
19 Very small
20 Open-textured fabric
23 Classifieds
24 Drapery ornament
25 Rivulet
27 "__ go bragh!"
29 Takes on
32 Impact sound
35 Twist
38 Actor Russell
39 Boxing bigwig
40 Bookworm, maybe
43 Disgusted expression
44 Resort place
46 Actress Braga
47 In favor of
48 Subway coins
51 Younger Guthrie
53 Free
56 Seasonal songs
60 Coolidge, for short
62 Seeking favor
64 Texas landmark
66 Israeli dance
67 Olympian Korbut
68 Skinflint
69 Scandinavian king

70 Likely MTV viewer
71 Nuisances
72 Try out
73 Med. personnel

DOWN
1 Show one's feelings
2 Oahu greeting
3 Decreases
4 Cutting on a slant
5 Grand work
6 Marsh ducks
7 Spartan slave
8 Used the tub
9 Had a bite
10 Used-car descriptor
11 Good-natured

12 Articulates
14 Reagan appointee
21 Suit fabric
22 __-la-la
26 Response from space
28 Henpecks
30 Peter, Paul and Mary, e.g.
31 Occupational suffix
32 Angler's worms
33 In addition
34 Translucent tableware
36 Greek consonant
37 Actress Olin
41 Copters and fighters

42 __ Lama
45 Always, to Keats
49 Gomer Pyle portrayer
50 Letters after R
52 "Ready __, here I come!"
54 *Some Like __*
55 Swiped
57 Eyed excessively
58 German weapon
59 Extends across
60 Army outpost
61 "I cannot tell __"
63 Memorable times
65 Encountered

25 LISTENING IN

by Shirley Soloway

ACROSS

1 Out of control
5 Cooking odor
10 Russian ruler
14 On the ocean
15 Very cold
16 Lhasa __
17 Close by
19 Art __
20 Not so hot
21 Daredevil Knievel
22 NASA affirmative
23 Wine valley
25 Sharp answers
28 Curved line
31 __ *Pass* (Uris novel)
33 Mr. Kabibble
34 *On __ Pond* ('81 film)
36 Wartime signal
40 Duel tool
41 Bit of bread
43 __ *Camera* ('55 film)
44 Come back
46 Father goose?
48 Down Under jumper
49 Physician of antiquity
51 Retirees' org.
52 Letting up
55 Objectives
57 __-relief
58 French river
60 Very fancy headgear
64 *A Farewell to __*
66 Oxymoronic display
68 Boxing event

69 First name in cosmetics
70 Unlikely to attack
71 Griffith or Rooney
72 Strict
73 Sp. ladies

DOWN

1 Desire
2 "Oh!"
3 Ballet move
4 Singer Bobby
5 Rep.
6 Use the microwave
7 Norwegian monarch
8 Ores, e.g.
9 Shake up
10 Smidgen
11 Leads the way
12 Wide neckwear
13 Corner chess pieces
18 "There Is Nothin' Like __"
24 __-nez
26 Start of a pencil game
27 K.T. of country music
28 Worry, perhaps
29 Use a lariat
30 Totally confusing
32 Gene Tierney thriller
35 Station
37 U.S. Grant's rank
38 Iowa college town
39 __ avis
42 Most tattered
45 Luau dish
47 ". . . __ all a good night"
50 Unwelcome admirer?
52 Addis __
53 Nobleman
54 Short messages
56 Prepares flour
59 Fill to the gills
61 Unlatched, maybe
62 Capital of *Italia*
63 Yes votes
65 Hog home
67 DC figure

26 GO-GETTERS

by David Owens

ACROSS

1 Nickname for Hemingway
5 Lhasa __
9 One at __ (singly)
14 Declare
15 Jungle home
16 Horse papas
17 How go-getters go
20 *Our Miss Brooks* star
21 Spirited session?
22 Popeye's girl
23 Cots on wheels
24 They may be split
28 Sting
30 Swamp
32 Seer's asset
33 __ facto
37 What go-getters do
40 Eye problem
41 Detective story pioneer
42 Ceremony
43 Stir up
45 Trunk
46 Shore specialty
50 Kimono cummerbund
52 Bays
53 Blackens
58 What go-getters have, with "a"
60 Lilting syllables
61 Egotist's obsession
62 Commedia dell'__
63 Parisian legislature
64 __-European
65 Misplace

DOWN

1 Wan
2 Tel __
3 Moplike pooch
4 Region
5 "Luck Be __" ('50 tune)
6 Den wood
7 Autograph
8 Poetic eye
9 State
10 Big fellow
11 Actress Dunne
12 Clemency
13 Snaky shapes
18 Concerto __ (musical form)
19 Coup leader
23 Deep cut
24 Rock-band equipment
25 Recommend
26 Air France destination
27 Gander or cob
29 Rhythm
31 Postulate
33 "Tell __ the judge!"
34 Rain hard
35 Aerobics centers
36 Scandinavian city
38 Frog kin
39 Protests that went nowhere?
43 Phrasal conjunction
44 Germanic gnome
46 Winnows
47 Acclimate
48 Comic __ Sherman
49 *The Most Happy __*
51 Smashing, á la *Variety*
53 Paradise
54 Slanted type: Abbr.
55 Goose egg
56 Gobbles up
57 Hook's henchman
59 "Unaccustomed __ am . . ."

by Shirley Soloway

ACROSS

1 Actress Virna
5 Belief
10 Garage item
14 Ken of *thirtysomething*
15 Daily delivery
16 Author Ferber
17 Auto maker
18 Sharon of Israel
19 Citric sips
20 Crusader symbol
23 I-beam material
24 Show pique
27 Performed diligently
31 Exploding stars
33 Tiny speck
36 Mohair producers
39 Eye area
41 More mirthful
42 Insect eggs
43 Tightly-curled fur
46 Caustic substance
47 Went awry
48 '50s Ford
50 Opera performers
53 Thompson or Hawkins
57 Chang and Eng
61 Singer Adams
64 Director Lean
65 Solidifies
66 Letterman rival
67 Graff of *Mr. Belvedere*
68 Folklore heavy
69 Fall faller
70 Sportscaster Merlin
71 Lunchtime

DOWN

1 Weavers' needs
2 __ ease (uncomfortable)
3 Edge along
4 Shoe part
5 IRS men
6 Uncommon
7 De Mille specialty
8 Horned animals
9 Synthetic fabric
10 Kitchen measure
11 Unusual
12 *A Chorus Line* number
13 *Viva __ Vegas*
21 Fitzgerald of jazz
22 Vocalized
25 Be of use
26 Shabby
28 Actress Swenson
29 Actor Richard
30 Holmes' creator
32 To be: Lat.
33 Con
34 In the open
35 __ Haute, IN
37 Peruse
38 Arsenal supplies
40 Have __ (understand)
44 __ *Do!* (Mary Martin musical)
45 Top-of-the-line
49 Sofa style
51 Dashboard feature
52 Little
54 San __, CA
55 Prelim
56 German city
58 Arden and namesakes
59 __ qua non
60 Genesis locale
61 Building wing
62 Poor grade
63 __ way (sort of)

by Shirley Soloway

ACROSS
1 Bible book
5 Avant-__
10 Last word in church
14 "__ Be Cruel" ('56 tune)
15 UFO pilot
16 Willing
17 Diva rendition
18 Sire
19 Theater sign
20 Visible to the naked eye
23 __ a *Wonderful Life*
24 Nasty smile
25 Summer TV shows
27 Visored hat
30 Reprimands
33 Likens
38 Archie's wife
39 Czech river
40 Big box
43 Art Deco designer
44 Cancellations
46 Came to a halt
48 Financial recipient
51 Dover's st.
52 Firefly, for one
54 Actress Emma
59 Texas coll.
61 Ethnically diverse
64 Mexican snack
66 Actor Reginald
67 __ avis
68 "Diana" singer
69 Rub out
70 "__ the Mood for Love"
71 Chivalrous deed

72 Methods: Abbr.
73 Forgo the fettuccine

DOWN
1 Photographer Ansel
2 Erin of *Happy Days*
3 In reserve
4 Gaze intently
5 Chews the fat
6 Actor Guinness
7 Austerity
8 More profound
9 Whole
10 Make cheddar better
11 Full-length garment

12 Send out
13 Fishing devices
21 Largest dolphin
22 Sugar shape
26 Artistic subjects
28 Rainbow shape
29 For each
31 Diminutive suffix
32 Lean-to
33 Viet __
34 Nasal appraisal
35 Big money
36 Disposed
37 In a blue mood
41 Slugger Williams
42 Compass letters

45 Sunflower support
47 *Casablanca* character
49 Classical pieces
50 Queen of mystery
53 Lab burners
55 Pungent
56 Orange Bowl's home
57 Donny's sister
58 Lean
59 Bambi's father
60 Horse hair
62 *Meet Me __ Louis*
63 Deli breads
65 Cereal grain

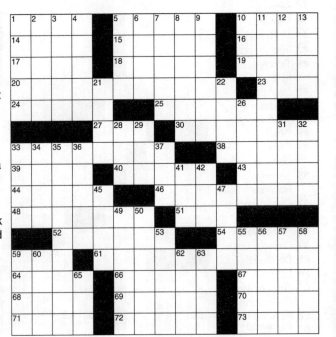

ENVELOPE, PLEASE

by Randolph Ross

ACROSS

1 Bates or King
5 Johnny's successor
8 He ran against Bill and George
12 Shade of green
13 Lennon's wife
14 Jacob's wife et al.
15 Envelope info
18 Before, to Byron
19 A Bobbsey twin
20 Examines the books
21 Former US territory
22 Silent okay
23 Patina
27 Invitees
31 Envelope info
33 *Exodus* protagonist
34 Dundee denial
35 Anger
36 Envelope info
43 Finish behind
44 Neatens (up)
45 Southern constellation
46 "What Kind of Fool __?"
47 Lay __ (disprove)
50 Motel freebie
51 Bread spread
54 Envelope handlers
57 Sends
58 Diamond __

59 Traffic-light color
60 Sentence part: Abbr.
61 Pinky or Peggy
62 Fabricated

DOWN

1 Orchard spray
2 Ade flavor
3 "__ Maria"
4 Newborn
5 Bennett or Blondell
6 Plus
7 Jedi instructor
8 Occupant
9 Kiln
10 Mother and daughter
11 Compass pt.
12 Washington bill
14 Ushered, perhaps
16 Muslim ascetic
17 Ladder steps
21 Small amount
23 Cabinet item
24 Forgets
25 *Hook* pooch
26 Flying pests
28 Grab
29 Garr and Copley
30 Dance movement
31 Salt, to a chemist
32 Serious

37 Two-__ (tot)
38 Emphasis
39 Breakfast bread
40 __ against time
41 M, C, or I
42 Half of MCCII
47 Autocratic ruler
48 Mayberry boy
49 Lofty
50 Dot in the sea
51 Be in harmony
52 Served well
53 Sea, to Seurat
54 Strike caller
55 First head of the UN
56 Old Dominion campus: Abbr.

ACROSS

1 Fizzy drink
5 Inclined planes
10 __ *Man Flint*
13 Ring results
14 Napoleon's fate
15 Western Indians
17 Work units
18 Snake poison
19 Prepares leather
20 Pol. contributor
21 Dairy container
23 Sorrowful word
25 Neither fish __ fowl
26 Gas ratings
29 Imitator
33 Cabdrivers
34 Hammers and saws
36 Long follower
37 Arthur of tennis
38 Make tapestries
39 Approve
40 Hwy.
41 *Being __* (Sellers film)
42 Fancy flapjack
43 Spray-can contents
45 Brushed off
47 Lass' counterpart
48 Bear in the stars
49 Blades on snow
55 Explosive: Abbr.
58 Inventor Elias
59 Lacks
60 Do a slow burn
61 Nights before
62 Public persona
63 Art __ ('20s style)

64 Superlative suffix
65 Carried around
66 Ticks off

DOWN

1 __ on it (hurry)
2 Pod veggie
3 Pound employee
4 Pack animal
5 Correct errors, e.g.
6 Ice skater's move
7 Wrap fur
8 Drop noisily
9 Florida collegian
10 Strong protest
11 Idaho neighbor

12 Descartes of math
16 Ukraine, formerly: Abbr.
21 "__ inhumanity to . . ."
22 Spinning toys
24 Blue spot on a map
26 Scarlett's maiden name
27 Social stratum
28 Foundry output
29 Sheltered places
30 Baker's material
31 With dropped jaw
32 Played cat and mouse
35 Canoe propeller

38 Novel genre
39 Heavenly bodies
41 Russian ruler
42 Scoundrels
44 Firstborn
46 Cared for
49 __ *Stoops to Conquer*
50 Tennis term
51 Lambs' moms
52 Verne character
53 In apple-pie order
54 Barely defeat
56 Bottle part
57 Ark complement
60 "Star Wars" defense program: Abbr.

31 BODY PAINTING

by Fred Piscop

ACROSS
1 Piece of candy
5 SASE, for one
9 Tower of __
14 __ Man (Estevez film)
15 Spanish surrealist
16 Tabletop decoration
17 Give __ (care)
18 Music genre
19 __ und Drang
20 Military decoration
23 Language suffix
24 Cause by necessity
25 Egyptian amulet
27 CO clock setting
29 Blob
32 Liver, for one
36 Bar mitzvah dance
39 New York college
40 Phone line
41 Norton's workplace
42 __ War (1899-1902)
43 Having color
44 __-Lease Act
45 "... I __ my way"
46 "__ by Starlight"
48 Hockey great Bobby
50 __ a pin
53 Some navels
58 The __ Four (Beatles)

60 Coward
62 Mount the soapbox
64 Goalie's success
65 Dresden denial
66 Kitchen gadget
67 Radio message-ender
68 Aware of
69 It __ a Thief
70 Waterman's wares
71 "A friend in __ ..."

DOWN
1 Window embellishment
2 Nick-at-Nite offering
3 Dizzying designs
4 Where's __? ('70 film)
5 '50s Fords
6 Lye, chemically
7 Crossword listings
8 Pale lavender
9 Small café
10 Picnic pest
11 Aristocrat
12 Wall features?
13 Old __, CT
21 Outline in detail
22 M*A*S*H role
26 Suspect's explanation
28 Quaker pronoun
30 "Dedicated to the __ Love"
31 Thespian's gig
32 Protest singer Phil

33 Beat decisively
34 Legal tender
35 Mix up
37 Have title to
38 Make over
41 Nominee listing
45 Beat decisively
47 Hens, e.g.
49 Galleon crew
51 Journalist Joseph
52 Drudge
54 Mortise mate
55 Actress Graff
56 Top-class
57 Church council
58 Army outpost
59 Opera solo
61 Pizzeria need
63 Placekicker's prop

32 LOVE AND KISSES

by Shirley Soloway

ACROSS

1 School org.
4 Western height
8 Faux __
11 Word of woe
12 Asia's __ Sea
13 In any way
16 Mattress partner
18 Sitcom actress Roker
19 Book issue
20 Women warriors
22 __-mo replay
23 Heavy metal
24 Butter bit
25 Forbid
28 Not fooled by
30 Have a snack
32 "He's making __ and checking . . ."
34 Very annoying
38 Alluring
39 Actor Bean
40 Poker stake
41 Absolve from blame
43 Political ploy
44 Leningrad's river
45 Sailor's patron
47 __ Na Na
48 Lwyr.
50 Roman roadway
52 Mel of baseball
54 Church section
56 Lure
60 Go __ (deteriorate)
61 Sporting dogs
63 Singer Cara
64 Not active
65 Apple center
66 Pregrown grass
67 __-do-well
68 Naval off.

DOWN

1 Trudge
2 Car for hire
3 Office aides: Abbr.
4 Leave stranded
5 Ireland's nickname
6 __ Jose, CA
7 Pond growth
8 Logical contradiction
9 From __ (completely)
10 Jazz instruments
11 "Honest" nickname
14 Director Wertmuller
15 "__ we forget"
17 Boeing captain
21 Massenet opera
23 Popular seafood
25 Infield corner
26 Emcee Trebek
27 Watergate focus
29 Synagogue scroll
31 *The King and I* setting
33 "Auld Lang __"
35 Christmas carol
36 Mormons' mecca
37 Antitoxins
39 Make a speech
42 Forced to vacate
43 __ voce
46 __ superior (nuns' boss)
48 Play's start
49 Thunder god
51 Spritelike
53 Cessation of hostilities
55 Forbidden act
56 Wheel connector
57 After a while
58 Superiors of 68 Across: Abbr.
59 Mao __-tung
62 Keats creation

33 ALL BUSINESS

by A.J. Santora

ACROSS

1 Lhasa __
5 "Phooey!"
8 Hair styles
13 Mythical birds
14 Tony-winner Merkel
15 Get in
16 Business-acquisition specialist
19 Company's tactic against 16 Across
20 Shooter ammo
21 Irritate
22 Bar crawler
23 Reproduce
25 Actor Voight
26 After expenses
28 __ polloi
29 Goes after apples
30 Prefix for physics
34 Building addition
35 Ogle
36 EMT technique
38 Selfish sort
39 "The __ Were"
41 Legal attachment
42 Plug's place
43 Psychic power
45 Little devil
46 Script direction
47 Mimic
49 Thompson of *Howards End*
51 Five-centime piece
52 Prey for 16 Across
57 Exec's insurance against 16 Across
58 Fabled Chicagoan
59 Adams or Ameche
60 Spanish 101 verb
61 Ruses
62 Chang's brother
63 Pentagram

DOWN

1 Compass drawings
2 Express contempt
3 In a gutsy way
4 Sea bird
5 Puppeteer Tillstrom
6 Microorganism
7 Women's weapons
8 Russian river
9 Men of the cloth
10 __ harm (was innocuous)
11 Runner Steve
12 Rev.'s recital
15 "Get Happy" composer
17 __ deal (initiate business)
18 Fish with a charge
23 Eat properly
24 Alley Oop's gal
25 Bliss
27 Have coming
29 Honey bunch
31 *Teahouse of __ Moon*
32 Thoroughfare
33 Monster
36 Ferber novel
37 Vitality
40 Work time for many
41 Citrus cooler
44 Garden flower
46 "__ a jolly good fellow"
47 Reef + lagoon
48 Word form for "old"
50 Sports award
51 Anatomical pouch
53 Users: Suff.
54 Sharp flavor
55 Singer James
56 Lacerate
57 House party: Abbr.

ACROSS

1 Ship's dock
5 In flames
10 Demeanor
14 Concerning
15 Carnival features
16 __-European (prototypical language)
17 Boy Scout beginner
19 Chem. and bio.
20 Sharon of Israel
21 Actress Lanchester
22 "__ went thataway!"
23 Riddle, e.g.
25 Melt
27 Marvin or Grant
28 Search for
31 Meadow males
34 Sincere
37 Happy
38 __ Baba
39 Fast cars
41 Atlas page
42 Taco topping
44 Prerecord
45 Capri, for one
46 Assumption
48 Dancer Miller
50 Pepper's partner
51 Wipes off
54 Makes believe
56 Alda of *M*A*S*H*
59 Stacked up
61 Winnie the __
62 Railroad boss
64 Sound of mind
65 Spread joy
66 Carryall
67 Bullfight bravos
68 Writer Runyon
69 Alps surface

DOWN

1 Pocket bread
2 Not moving
3 Comic Kovacs
4 Distributes again
5 Airport info: Abbr.
6 Drummer's companion
7 Role model
8 Early autos
9 Large homestead
10 Faux pas
11 Little crawlers
12 Singer Adams
13 Prone to snoop
18 Otherwise
24 Architect Saarinen
26 Alters pants
28 Hog food
29 Russian range
30 Use a keyboard
31 Scraping sound
32 Winglike
33 Major step
35 Diminutive ending
36 Coach Parseghian
39 Solid rain
40 Costly
43 Breaks to bits
45 Won't budge
47 Remained
49 Wine valley
51 Put an __ (stop)
52 Rock singer __ John
53 Take care of
54 Lhasa __ (dog)
55 Heat source
57 "Ooh __!"
58 Composer Khachaturian
60 Made a sketch
63 Half the honeymooners

by Eric Albert

ACROSS
1 Fast-food favorite
7 Shipmate of Jason
15 Shrewd-minded
16 Musical chestnut
17 English essayist
19 Betelgeuse, e.g.
20 Half of dos
21 Tiny circle
24 Thesaurus name
26 Sleeve fold
30 Not cool
33 Pooh pal's signature
34 Unimportant
35 In coastal Maine
37 Diverse
38 Famous sharpshooter
40 Chore
42 King David, for one
45 Feminist Friedan
46 Distress signal
47 __ Barbara, CA
48 Foundation
49 In a lather
51 Swindle
52 A ways away
53 Geezer
56 *Evening Shade* actress
64 Short piano piece
65 Split
66 Filament element
67 Tomboy

DOWN
1 Cave flier
2 Adjective ending
3 Racing-car initials
4 "__ the word!"
5 Rat-__
6 Señor Chavez
7 Inspire wonder in
8 Actress Welch
9 Sow sound
10 Buckeye State
11 Nantes negative
12 Bow line?
13 Manipulate
14 Mystery writer Josephine
18 Nod off
21 Defective bomb
22 Yoko __
23 Stymies
25 Degenerate
26 The pix biz
27 Eternal
28 Pro
29 Cook bacon
31 Natural-born
32 Candy cost, once
34 Cogitates
36 Help out
37 Jamaican music
39 In itself
40 Flow back
41 Stephen of *The Crying Game*
43 Pigpen
44 Phone bug
46 Undisturbed
49 Nun's wear
50 Fish unofficially
52 Thomas Waller
54 Skagerrak seaport
55 He and she
56 W. Va. setting
57 "Skip to My __"
58 Hostelry
59 Move at a sharp angle
60 Brown shade
61 Stripling
62 *All About __*
63 Strong longing

36 OUT WITH THE OLD

by Shirley Soloway

ACROSS

1 Purchase price
5 Egg-shaped
10 Movie terrier
14 Opera solo
15 __ apparent reason
16 Sgts., for example
17 Balers' tools
19 Get bigger
20 Perfectly
21 Fill up
23 Upperclassman: Abbr.
24 Reading and B&O
26 Low down
27 Like some stomachs
30 Four-poster, for instance
33 Add up to
36 Shoshoneans
37 Dover __ (fish)
38 "__ to the wise . . ."
39 Review badly
40 Got up
41 Not so much
42 Composer Porter
43 Croissant creator
44 Asner and Wynn
45 Small carpet
47 Poet Teasdale
49 Bro's sibling
50 Impersonate
53 Out-and-out
56 Starts a tennis point
58 French composer
59 Dinner entree
62 Author Hunter
63 Ghostlike
64 Tiny creature
65 Boggs of baseball
66 Golfer Sam
67 Otherwise

DOWN

1 Marvel and America: Abbr.
2 Mythical hunter
3 Shankar's instrument
4 Social asset
5 Proposes
6 "Hinky Dinky Parlay __"
7 Bobby of hockey
8 Prepares the presses
9 Square-dance call
10 Ms. Dickinson
11 Clippings holder
12 Horn sound
13 ". . . have mercy on such __"
18 Miami paper
22 __ *Little Indians*
25 Dazed state
27 Traffic jammers
28 Author Calvino
29 Extends a subscription
31 Actress Sommer
32 Forest forager
33 Anecdote
34 Had a debt
35 Dinner preparation step
37 Pirate's haul
40 One who mistreats
42 "__ Are" (Mathis tune)
45 Singer's syllable
46 Took a chance
48 Repent
50 Make use of
51 Annoyances
52 Lauder of lipstick
53 Used a bubble pipe
54 Volcanic flow
55 Afterwards
57 Capital of Italy
60 Noun suffix
61 FBI's counterpart

37 PHASES OF THE MOON

by Dean Niles

ACROSS

1 Bide one's time
5 Eng. honor
8 Lawn growth
13 __ of Green Gables
14 __ and crafts
16 Hair-care activity
17 Harplike instrument
18 __ as a button
19 Reference list
20 Porky features
23 Three __ match
24 Southern sch.
25 Spills the beans
30 Pie piece
32 Turnstile opening
34 All __ (listening)
35 Literary collection
37 Nigerian town
38 Conclusions
39 Fanatical group
43 Cartel: Abbr.
44 Mork's home
45 Many mos.
46 "Somebody bet __ bay"
47 Role for Stack
49 With an __ (in consideration of)
53 Wifely
55 Preserve, as fruit
57 Geometry proof letters
58 Debussy piece
61 __ the Hutt (Star Wars series villain)
65 Sports org.
66 Whence sunrise is seen
67 Outsider
68 Edward Scissorhands star
69 Rescind a correction
70 Give rise to
71 Ready to go
72 Antitoxins

DOWN

1 Luxuriate
2 "__ Can Whistle"
3 Progress
4 High-schooler
5 Miracle on 34th Street store
6 Caesar's addressee
7 Caesar's question
8 Ground grain
9 __ Tin Tin
10 Here __ now
11 Point farthest from NNW
12 Dr. Ruth topic
15 Placed in the mail
21 Actress Verdugo
22 Mel's Diner, e.g.
26 Very small
27 "Auld __ Syne"
28 Earth: Ger.
29 Draft grp.
31 Male goose
33 Last __ (final at-bat)
36 Like some modern music
39 Bobcat
40 Negate
41 Limerick location
42 Cara of Fame
43 Old French coin
48 Difficult situation
50 Draw a parallel
51 More wound up
52 Folk-blues singer
54 "__ Get Started"
56 Adjust to conditions
59 Readies champagne
60 Negative suffix
61 Boxer's motion
62 Dark malt
63 Tom Hanks film
64 Stinging insect

38 SPEAK UP!

by Shirley Soloway

ACROSS

1 Adored one
5 Heavenly instrument
9 *Leave __ Beaver*
13 Neck part
14 Screenwriter James
15 Love, in Lille
16 Claire and Balin
17 Rickey requirement
18 Boxing arenas
19 Speak the truth
22 Map close-up
23 Stephen of *The Crying Game*
24 Suction tube
27 More briny
31 "__ Blue?"
32 Proportions
36 Singer Fitzgerald
37 Chatter on and on
40 Richard of films
41 Swamp creatures, for short
42 Insect egg
43 Pours a second cup, perhaps
45 Jane and Edmund
47 Casual shirt
48 War horse
51 Say something nice
57 *The Lady __*
58 Temperate
59 He loved Irish Rose
60 Sky lights?
61 "Ye __ Gift Shoppe"
62 Take a nap
63 May celebrants
64 Wintertime vehicle
65 Changes colors

DOWN

1 "What's __ for me?"
2 Victor Borge was one
3 Milky gemstone
4 Actor __ Howard
5 Brings to a stop
6 Nimble
7 Send in payment
8 Take a look
9 Did a takeoff on
10 Singer Tennille
11 Pulls hard
12 Hosp. areas
15 Sharon of Israel
20 Opening bars
21 Mistake remover
24 Latin dad
25 Reflection
26 Rice style
27 London neighborhood
28 Massey of the movies
29 Pixieish
30 River transports
33 Fisherman
34 Afternoon socials
35 Novel ending?
38 Sweater makers
39 Made a request
44 Yorkshire city
46 Playwright Albee
48 Ability
49 The squiggle in "señor"
50 Came to a close
51 "Do __ others . . ."
52 Mine car
53 Noted cookie maker
54 Follow orders
55 Get up
56 P.D. investigators
57 Doctrine

39 LITTLE CIRCLES

by Wayne R. Williams

ACROSS
1 Night-sky sight
5 Jacob's brother
9 Not suitable
14 Sky bear
15 __ best friend
16 Showy flower
17 Halfway into a flight
20 Regulations
21 Menu item
22 Comparative ending
23 Protuberance
24 Wheels around
28 Gregory Hines specialty
29 River projects
33 Small, brownish antelope
34 Shaped like a rainbow
36 Night flyer
37 Historical-movie requirement
40 Traveler's stop
41 Static
42 Composer Erik
43 Relative of "great" and "keen"
45 TV hardware
46 Bit of food
47 Alternative to a saber
49 Name a knight
50 Not noticed
53 Maladies
58 Computer-printer technology
60 Bay window
61 Pennsylvania port
62 South American nation
63 Reddish-brown quartzes
64 Neckline shapes
65 Air pollution

DOWN
1 Has dinner
2 Horse's pace
3 The largest continent
4 Declaim violently
5 Overacts
6 Morley of *60 Minutes*
7 Jillian and Beattie
8 GI entertainers
9 Overturn
10 Caught fish, in a way
11 Bridge quorum
12 Concerning
13 Newcastle's river
18 School fee
19 Examine a case again
23 Mother-of-pearl
24 Arrive unexpectedly
25 Goddess of peace
26 Actress __ Lisi
27 Kimono sash
28 Reliance
30 Borders on
31 Scientist Curie
32 Drum or wool material
34 Burning
35 Fail to heed
38 Museum guide
39 Old sailor
44 Came down in buckets
46 Rumples
48 Rings out
49 Southern anthem
50 Japanese vegetables
51 Writer Ephron
52 Be up and about
53 Ominous
54 Poisonous snakes
55 Part of a pipe
56 Architect Saarinen
57 Self-satisfied
59 Gun the motor

GIVE UP?

by Shirley Soloway

ACROSS

1 Attired
5 Mary's pet
9 Entertainers
14 Conceal
15 Iris layer
16 Kukla's pal
17 Up above
18 Price
19 Actress Davis
20 SURRENDER
23 Have a feeling about
24 Wine region of Italy
25 Boulevard liners
28 Rooftop structure
33 Swelled head
36 Counts calories
39 __ Romeo (car)
40 SURRENDERS
44 Actor Richard
45 Firm
46 Dads of Jrs.
47 Make a choice
50 Forget to include
52 Sound like a snake
55 Characteristic
59 SURRENDER
65 More or less
66 Cleo's river
67 TV handyman
68 Washer cycle
69 Church area
70 Roman road
71 Runs into
72 Have a strong odor
73 Respond rudely

DOWN

1 Converses casually
2 Graceful
3 Add embellishment
4 Put out of power
5 Lynda Bird's sister
6 Stratford's river
7 Hostess Perle
8 Washups
9 Render immobile
10 Butter alternative
11 Did in
12 Utensil point
13 Circus star
21 Attaches permanently
22 Greek vowel
26 Farrow of *Zelig*
27 Takes up a hem
29 Brit. flyers
30 Troubles
31 Distant, to Donne
32 Falls behind
33 Farm females
34 Redcoat general
35 Egg-shaped
37 However, for short
38 Grain housing
41 Chemical suffix
42 Comic Conway
43 Archie's mate
48 Skydivers' needs
49 Gratuity
51 Country singer Randy
53 Submarine system
54 Take potshots at
56 O'Day or Baker
57 Runs without moving
58 Ivan and Peter
59 Cause damage to
60 Theater award
61 Solitary
62 Homemaker's nemesis
63 "What __ is new?"
64 Look for

41 LONG TIME

by Wayne R. Williams

ACROSS

1 Fill too tightly
5 *M*A*S*H* star
9 Tint
14 Protagonist
15 Dates
16 Atelier item
17 Long time
20 Track official
21 Hatcher of *Lois & Clark*
22 Park art
25 Flairs
30 Strike sharply
32 "The Raven" lady
33 Existed
36 Saudis, e.g.
38 Khatami's land
39 Long time
43 Gold patch
44 Prefix for "sun"
45 Compass dir.
46 Puts up
49 Blockheads
51 Relatives of roads
53 Boat building area
57 Carpenter's need
59 French brother
60 Long time
66 Garden area
67 Hurries
68 Pennsylvania port
69 Rider's straps
70 Woodcutters
71 Mtg.

DOWN

1 Confabs
2 Send payment
3 Lure of the kitchen
4 Some Impressionist paintings
5 Volcanic dust
6 August sign
7 Quick and skillful
8 Selling feature
9 Doddering
10 Possessed
11 Simile center
12 Susan of *L.A. Law*
13 Loop trains
18 Author Capote
19 Russian river
23 Ireland
24 Hidden supply
26 Novelist Bagnold
27 Ephron and others
28 TV dinner holders
29 Significance
31 Dropped back
33 Hand signals
34 Paying attention
35 More crafty
37 Met show-stoppers
40 Fairy-tale opener
41 Small brook
42 Let know
47 Domingo and Pavarotti, e.g.
48 Laurel or Getz
50 Spending frenzies
52 Indian sect members
54 "__ the World"
55 *Mrs. __ Goes to Paris*
56 Affirmative comments
58 *Star Wars* princess
60 A ways away
61 Mine find
62 Diamond stat
63 Put on
64 Evergreen tree
65 Draft letters

by Shirley Soloway

ACROSS

1 Only
5 Figure-skater Thomas
9 The Devil
14 Related
15 *The Good Earth* character
16 Novelist Zola
17 Sail support
18 Shuttle org.
19 Pee Wee of baseball
20 Somehow
23 Agree
24 Trimmed of fat
25 P.I.
27 __ *Rides Again*
32 Make changes to
36 Put on board
39 Opera highlight
40 Somehow
43 Ireland's alias
44 And others: Abbr.
45 Carries on
46 Stretching muscle
48 Lamb's mom
50 Rugged rock
53 "__ Fideles"
58 Somehow
63 Weekly pay
64 Underground growth
65 Mandlikova of tennis
66 __ a minute (fast)
67 Tommy of Broadway
68 Manages, with "out"
69 Baseballer Staub
70 Impersonated
71 Learning method

DOWN

1 Latin dance
2 Rubber-stamps
3 Shopping aids
4 __ nous (confidentially)
5 Contribute
6 Israeli airline
7 Kind of metabolism
8 Senseless
9 Cool and calm
10 From the U.S.
11 Stadium row
12 In addition
13 __-do-well
21 Opening bars of music
22 Mommy's mate
26 Coagulate
28 Roosevelt matriarch
29 Disney film of '82
30 Hilarious performance
31 Beasts of burden
32 Support
33 Stringed instrument of yore
34 Lacking substance
35 Many centuries
37 ". . . man __ mouse?"
38 Talented
41 Tralee's county
42 Belief
47 Dramatist Sean
49 Had a yen for
51 The main artery
52 Aggregation
54 Anesthetic
55 Military headwear
56 Doctrine
57 Rub out
58 Man __ (racehorse)
59 __, *the Killer Whale* ('66 film)
60 Sponsorship
61 Shoe part
62 Tiptop

43 CREATURE FEATURE

by Cathy Millhauser

ACROSS

1 Door post
5 Polite address
10 Do one's part?
14 *Siegfried* solo
15 Mrs. Kramden
16 Milky gem
17 Sugar source
18 Wallace family's *The Book of __*
19 Inclination to anger
20 What the over-the-hill man had?
23 Sneaker need
24 Least well
25 Mock
28 "Super!"
30 Elvis' middle name
31 Kid's sandwich leftover
32 AWOL pursuers
35 What the man who jumped to conclusions had?
39 "For shame!"
40 Less than a man?
41 The Sundance Kid's girlfriend
42 Spherical hairstyles
43 One of Santa's team
45 Routine-bound
48 Florence's river
49 What the propmaster for *The Sting* had?
54 They're inflatable
55 Usage expert Newman

56 Losers of '45
58 "Rule Britannia" composer
59 British novelist Charles
60 Scout quarters
61 Overlook
62 Makes an appointment
63 Nervous

DOWN

1 Fast punch
2 Realm
3 Appearance
4 At war
5 "With __ toward none . . ."
6 Skirt shape
7 Meal choice
8 *Othello* opener
9 Superlatively sloppy
10 Blue shade
11 Put one's two cents in
12 Fountain orders
13 Hallow'd
21 Blue
22 *The Bell Jar* author
25 Cuckoo
26 Fouls up
27 Chess castle
28 Looks like Carroll's cat
29 Stratagem
31 "Ah" follower
32 Closet undesirable
33 Top of the head
34 Film rater's unit

36 Jestingly
37 Our hemisphere
38 Echo
42 Springs
43 Bagpipe sounds
44 Author Beattie
45 Car-suspension piece
46 Valentino's girlfriend
47 Ages
48 Stomach
50 Mother of invention?
51 Did the crawl
52 Marked a ballot
53 High-pitched sound
57 Hog's home

44 EURO MENU

by Carol Blumenstein

ACROSS

1 Tranquil
5 Knight's mount
10 __ up (support)
14 Culture medium
15 Rex Stout detective
16 Lanyard
17 Dinner veggies
20 In the dumps
21 Vigorous
22 Most despicable
23 Computer monitors: Abbr.
24 Rat (on)
25 Zodiacal bull
28 Out of __ (antiquated)
29 Fourth mo.
32 Felonious flames
33 Recipe word
34 Bassoon kin
35 Dark dessert
38 Spider's octet
39 A son of Zeus
40 Like most new movies
41 Ending for Japan or Siam
42 Iowa city
43 Sovereigns
44 Slipped
45 Mountain lion
46 Matches up
49 __ mater
50 Spanish article
53 Dinner starter
56 Peel
57 Go in
58 __ Karenina
59 Against All __ ('84 film)
60 Titles to property
61 Favorites

DOWN

1 Taxis
2 Site of the Taj Mahal
3 Praise
4 Title for a married woman
5 Exercise attire
6 For Whom the Bell __
7 Otherwise
8 Failing grades
9 Uses up
10 Sneak about
11 Cad
12 Makes a choice
13 Nuisance
18 Reduced
19 Word with play or model
23 Kin to gators
24 Appropriates
25 Put off
26 City on the Rhône
27 Custom
28 Acts riskily
29 Wane
30 Fireplace tool
31 Tall grasses
33 Not interested
34 City near Gainesville
36 Starved
37 Author Capote
42 Baldwin of The Getaway
43 Tabloid tidbits
44 Dispatches
45 Practiced (a trade)
46 '60s hairstyle
47 Grillwork
48 Rip
49 Poker stake
50 The __ Ranger
51 Family member
52 Health farms
54 __-armed bandit
55 Patsy

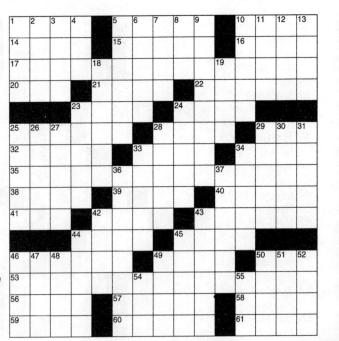

45 WAYS TO GO

by Robert H. Wolfe

ACROSS

1 Israeli port
6 *Bonanza* role
10 *The World According to* __
14 Visibly happy
15 Caron film of '53
16 On __ with (equivalent to)
17 Laissez __
18 Nudge a little
19 Nutmeg relative
20 High range
22 Go __ (fall apart)
24 Take time off
26 Jodie and Stephen
27 Light-dimming device
31 Percent ending
32 Negotiations
33 Carried
35 *Birth of a Nation* grp.
38 Perry's penner
39 Go __ (deteriorate)
40 Port, for one
41 Workout place
42 Pounce on prey
43 See-through
44 Nectar collector
45 Potluck dinner item
47 Expected
51 Old phone feature
52 "Go __!" (oath)
54 Covers a cutlet
58 The good earth
59 Sinful
61 Pang
62 Christian Science founder
63 Take a train
64 Spoiler
65 Thumbs-ups
66 Snow rider
67 __ on (incited)

DOWN

1 Sword handle
2 Gelatin ingredient
3 Mr. Nastase
4 Go __ (risk all)
5 Not impressed
6 Swiss height
7 Scuttlebutt
8 Unconcerned
9 Linear center
10 Reproductive cell
11 Swiftly
12 Souped-up auto
13 Conference questioners
21 DC clock setting
23 Key, for instance
25 Unmentionable
27 US 76 and CA 101, e.g.
28 A Marx instrument
29 "A-Tisket, A-Tasket" singer
30 *Fiddler on the Roof* star
34 Caught cattle
35 Chicken __
36 Baby bouncer
37 Lancaster's love in *From Here To Eternity*
39 Stamp collector's tool
40 Go __ (plunge in)
42 __ precedent
43 Do the unexpected
44 Budd and Bigelow
46 Don't play it straight
47 Cruising
48 Arlo's dad
49 Stand
50 New Jersey iceman
53 Faction
55 Cut __ (dance)
56 Medicinal amount
57 Tournament ranking
60 Guided

46 DRINK UP!

by Wayne R. Williams

ACROSS

1 Pepsi rival
5 "Home on the __"
10 Chair part
14 Norse god
15 Sacred images
16 Source of poi
17 Foundry form
18 "Night and Day" composer
20 Actress Dahl
22 Prehistoric
23 Flightless bird
24 Five-spot
26 Lab burners
27 Incur resentment
30 RN's specialty
31 Mr. Antony
32 Cellular substance: Abbr.
33 Director Eric
37 Dwight's nickname
38 Escape from prison
40 Actor Wallach
41 Tall buildings
43 Seabird
44 Hebrew letter
45 Ignited
46 Nevada attraction
48 Used a lariat
51 Writer Rand
52 Broadcast
53 Frozen regions
55 Horse's home
58 Snitch
61 "I've __ had!"
62 Nautical adverb
63 Fiction book
64 Allow to use
65 Orange-red mineral
66 Dirt path
67 Time periods

DOWN

1 Deep sleep
2 Aroma
3 Homer-hitter Harmon
4 Localized
5 Popular side dish
6 Fuss
7 Lon of Cambodia
8 Gather gradually
9 Sports cable network
10 Actress Elaine
11 Turn toward midnight
12 Show place
13 Law-school course
19 Spotted wildcat
21 Fanatic
24 Boggy grounds
25 In an angry way
27 Give off
28 Type of shark
29 Guardianship
30 Tree part
34 German composer
35 Novelist Kazan
36 Fruit covering
38 Wedding-related
39 Algerian seaport
42 Voted in
44 Friendly
47 Snack on
48 Moreno et al.
49 Central Florida city
50 An apostle
51 John Jacob __
54 Closely confined
55 Vend
56 Melodious Horne
57 Finishes up
59 Gardner of *Mogambo*
60 Maui garland

47 SCREEN SCORCHERS

by Frank Gordon

ACROSS

1 Demean
6 Cleverness
9 Forgoes food
14 Grand Prix entrant
15 Wedding words
16 Say
17 Kate's TV housemate
18 Just out
19 Writer Ephron et al.
20 Mel Brooks film
23 Misplace
24 Houston hitter
25 Indy 500 tally
27 Aliens: Abbr.
28 Weasel's sound?
29 Penn. neighbor
31 Me, to Maurice
32 Papas' partners
34 "__ a Grecian Urn"
36 '74 disaster film, with *The*
41 Egg shapes
42 Govt. security
43 Obtain
44 Printer's measures
47 Sot's affliction
48 DDE's command
51 Paris landmark
53 Santa __
55 "Put __ on it!"
56 Best Picture of '81
59 Stallone role
60 Rainy
61 Greek letters
62 Office-communication system
63 Corn portion
64 College women
65 Al __ (pasta specification)
66 Kind of martini
67 Bewildered

DOWN

1 Fit for farming
2 Voter's paper
3 In __ by itself (unique)
4 Impound
5 "... __ saw Elba"
6 Bird or plane measure
7 That is: Lat.
8 Facing
9 Endow
10 South Pacific feature
11 Party decoration
12 Recipe measure
13 Last year's jrs.
21 Singer Judd
22 Unknown John
26 Word form for "Chinese"
28 Analyze a sentence
30 Yuppie apartments
32 Actor Gibson
33 Cpl.'s superior
35 Billy __ Williams
36 Roman garb
37 Surmounted
38 Night worker
39 Business activity
40 Untrue
45 AT&T rival
46 Put on the brakes
48 Exclusive groups
49 Angry speech
50 Black Sea port
52 Nun's wear
54 On __ (rampaging)
55 "The game is __!"
57 Function
58 Pay-stub abbr.
59 Carpet color

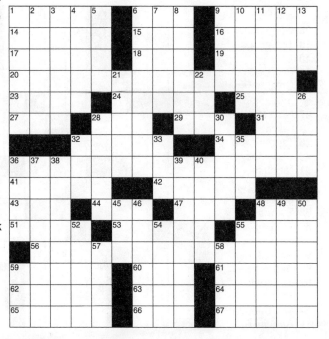

48 SHELL GAME

by Shirley Soloway

ACROSS

1 Fastener
6 Bit of dew
10 Fizzy fluid
14 Less tinted
15 Intense anger
16 Adam Arkin's dad
17 Too big
18 Prophetic sign
19 Minor damage
20 Decorative border
23 Is under the weather
24 Everyone
25 Western mount
29 Patella
33 Neutral shade
36 Actress Gabor
37 Catfish catchers
38 Coop critter
39 Yemeni port
40 __ jiffy
41 Cropped pants
45 Child protection
47 Nice and warm
48 Tapper Miller
49 Diplomacy
51 Nighttime working hours
57 Folk follower
58 Estrada of TV
59 Actress Patricia et al.
61 Always
62 Ready to eat
63 Fortuneteller's card
64 Ms. Trueheart
65 Require
66 Make a speech

DOWN

1 USN man
2 Chem. rooms
3 Guinness or Baldwin
4 Western sight
5 Bishop, e.g.
6 Salivate
7 Inclines
8 Curved molding
9 Necklace dangler
10 Riding seat
11 Cassini of design
12 Borge, e.g.
13 Picnic pest
21 Fabricator
22 Gen. Robert __
25 Kind of boom
26 Laughing mammal
27 "Swinging on __"
28 Aves.' kin
29 Good-natured
30 Yields
31 Turn away
32 Spring bloomer
34 "Huh?"
35 Garment bottom
39 Muslim ruler
41 100-yr. periods
42 Outdoor-party light
43 Annoying sensation
44 Penetrated
46 Duel tools
49 Worthless talk
50 Made a request
51 Be enamored of
52 Mine finds
53 Great Lake
54 Feeling of dread
55 Fictional estate
56 Narrow opening
57 Permit
60 Fr. holy woman

ACROSS
1 Drivel
4 Just fair
8 Electricity
13 Airline to Tokyo
14 Lab burner
15 Bower
16 Ancient harp
18 Composer Satie
19 Dolphins' home
20 Mrs. Trump, once
23 Pitcher Darling
24 A thousand G's
25 Delhi wrap
26 On the whole
29 Some G.I.'s
34 Chicago airport
35 Pea coats?
37 Jannings of *The Blue Angel*
38 Passé
39 Slangy suffix
40 Hersey bell town
41 Buffalo's lake
42 Ifs follower
43 Knight weapon
44 Roof type
46 Fishing boats
47 Actor Max
49 Hosp. staffers
50 Caveman Alley __
53 Hughes aircraft
58 Fork partner
60 Burden
61 Dog's bane
62 Kremlin name, once
63 Formal letter opening
64 Fond du __, WI
65 Vigilant
66 Rooney or Williams
67 Olive-tree relative

DOWN
1 Tropical tree
2 Writer Seton
3 Young salmon
4 Attractive
5 Other: Sp.
6 Small cuts
7 AL team
8 Overcrowds
9 Sch. in the smallest state
10 Steel beam
11 Singer Perry
12 Ireland
17 New Haven sights
21 Felt poorly
22 Cupid
26 Computer adjunct
27 Colleen Maureen
28 Participated
30 __ Lebanon
31 Muscat man
32 Pie choice
33 Blackthorns
35 *Bonanza* ranch
36 Ancient
40 "I'll String __ With You"
42 "I don't give __!"
45 Missing
46 Stylish
48 Argument
50 N. Mex. neighbor
51 Like Nash's lama
52 Yearn
54 Cheese lump
55 __ podrida
56 Briny septet
57 Apiece
59 Douglas __

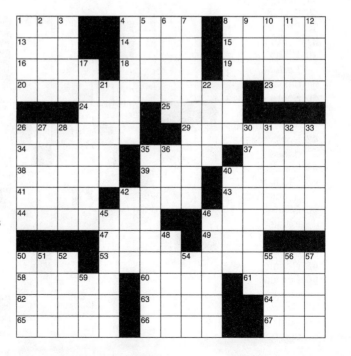

by Janie Lyons

ACROSS

1 Roseanne's former surname
5 Israeli native
10 Carpenter's tool
14 Mayberry moppet
15 Felt poorly
16 Appear
17 Hip '50s comic
19 Over with
20 Trial
21 Extra copies
23 Developed
25 Bad weather
26 Street noise
29 Donkey's uncle
31 Stiller's wife/partner
34 Nicholas, e.g.
35 Part of TGIF
36 Spanish city
37 __ Khan
38 *Wheel of Fortune*, basically
40 Scot's topper
41 Suppose, to Jed Clampett
43 Bobbysoxer's dance
44 Location
45 Old-time anesthetic
46 Civil War initials
47 Chinese cuisine
48 Negate
50 Political coalition
52 Treed
55 Foot components
59 Competent
60 *Family Affair* actor
62 Carol
63 In awe
64 Sea avian
65 Harper or Trueheart
66 Stockings stuff
67 *The Naked and the __*

DOWN

1 Western tie
2 Little or Frye
3 Melon leftover
4 Bridge botcher
5 Dark marten
6 Broadcast
7 Indistinct image
8 School break
9 Proficient
10 Had hopes
11 Ex-partner of Jerry Lewis
12 Pizazz
13 Ambulance personnel: Abbr.
18 Knitter's need
22 Type of type
24 Alert
26 Ogler's look
27 Map speck
28 R&B singer
30 Nostalgic sounds
32 Lasso
33 Commercial developers?
35 Ceiling device
36 Atlas page
38 Songstress Lena
39 Old kingdom
42 Dog sitters
44 Hit the top
46 Priests and bishops
47 Goose talk
49 Municipal
51 Napery
52 Defeatist's word
53 A woodwind
54 Watch part
56 Engage
57 Italian volcano
58 Backyard structure
61 GI's mail abbr.

51 INTERNATIONAL GAMES

by Fred Piscop

ACROSS

1 Polite forms of address
6 Cleanser brand
10 Ninnies
14 Cat's-eye relative
15 Paper quantity
16 Prima donna's tune
17 Board game
20 He can put you to sleep
21 New hire, perhaps
22 Singer James
24 Tire features
25 Rio Grande city
29 European coal region
31 Petri-dish stuff
32 Salt, chemically
34 Inventor Howe
39 High-risk game
42 Divs.
43 Wedding-cake part
44 Seward Peninsula city
45 Former Big Apple paper, for short
47 Made reparation
49 *Being and Nothingness* author
53 Sicilian spewer
55 Alexandra, for one
57 Two continents, collectively
62 Strength game
64 Jump
65 __-Contra hearings
66 Quickly, old-style
67 Messes up
68 Seeing things?
69 Rover

DOWN

1 Some Apples
2 Turkish title
3 Not "fer"
4 Obey
5 Appeared to be
6 Commentator Musburger
7 NRC predecessor
8 Bangkok coin
9 Sworn secrecy: It.
10 Comic actor Jack
11 Field of endeavor
12 Shot off
13 Envelope encls.
18 ". . . Muffet __ tuffet . . ."
19 Library cubicle
23 Attribute
25 Cooking fat
26 Fit of chills
27 File type
28 Prefix for while
30 Houseplant
33 Opposed
35 Letterman rival
36 *Blame __ Rio* ('84 film)
37 "Look __!" ("Pay attention!")
38 Tree-to-be
40 Adriatic peninsula
41 Planet discovered in 1781
46 Michael of *The Third Man*
48 Kilt design
49 Subway entrance
50 Grant portrayer
51 Nehi drinker
52 Loses footing
54 Most high-schoolers
56 Off-course
58 Fido fare
59 *The King and I* locale
60 Peruvian of yore
61 Made mellow
63 __ Dawn Chong

by Shirley Soloway

ACROSS

1 Jeanne d'___
4 Air attacks
9 Citrus drinks
13 Stinging remark
15 Cook's coverup
16 Ali ___
17 Concluded
18 Hidden character flaw
20 Jason's wife
22 Peter or Franco
23 Election winners
24 Loses control
28 Kingly address
29 Bag handles
33 Start of a Latin dance
36 Burdened beasts
39 Potpourri
40 Avoid
44 Brainstorm
45 Beauty establishment
46 However, for short
47 Feathered talker
50 Run off
52 Be cooperative
58 Ecological org.
61 Love, in León
62 ___ firma
63 "Get lost!"
67 April forecast
68 Clinton's veep
69 Soviet ruler
70 Normandy town
71 Walk heavily
72 Sidled

73 Inventor Whitney

DOWN

1 Manhattan Project result
2 *Bolero* composer
3 Statement of belief
4 Brit. pilots
5 Imitate
6 Actress Dunne
7 Is overfond
8 Responds derisively
9 Easy as ___
10 Spanish surrealist
11 Abba of Israel

12 Utters
14 Makes tea
19 A third of a yard
21 From China
25 Approximately
26 Makes a home
27 Ship's front
30 Landed
31 Solidity
32 London neighborhood
33 Computer element
34 "If I ___ Hammer"
35 State as fact
37 The Fabulous '50s, e.g.
38 Germ fighter

41 Crime fighter Wyatt
42 Univ. part
43 Genuflected
48 Oil of ___
49 Mexican food
51 Water holders
53 Harnessed
54 Take along
55 Angry
56 Singing style
57 Vietnam's capital
58 Quiche ingredients
59 Mosconi's game
60 '60s hairdo
64 Chicken part
65 Make a knot
66 Finale

53 FEATHER REPORT

by A.J. Santora

ACROSS
1 Shocked
7 Palindromic name
10 Grassy field
13 Comic Wil
14 Fort __, NJ
15 Co. name add-on
16 Walter Lantz character
19 Rubbing liq.
20 Bk. writer
21 Prefix for dynamics
22 __-do-well
24 "Poetry Man" singer
28 '90s music form
30 Phone sound
31 De-bunk?
33 "__ Fly Now" (Rocky theme)
35 Poor grade
38 Grisham bestseller
41 Dawn goddess
42 Court orders
43 Escapades
44 Many eras
45 Superlative suffix
46 DeVito role
52 Basics
55 First-class
56 Namedropper
58 Anger
59 Padres' mascot
64 Part of TNT
65 Caustic solution
66 Most breezy
67 Asner and Ames
68 Moon vehicle, for short
69 Accentuate

DOWN
1 __ in the Head (Sinatra film)
2 Supermarket stuff
3 Secreted
4 Writer Seton
5 Gain a monopoly
6 Faithfulness
7 Combine numbers
8 Fall a bit
9 Chopper's tool
10 Compare
11 January in Juarez
12 __ to pick (argumentation)
13 Aquatic bird
17 Exulter's cry
18 In any __ (regardless)
23 Grate
25 Lab burners
26 Cold-war capital
27 Permit
29 Small fry
31 Munched on
32 Greek letter
33 Readying for inspection
34 World Series mo.
35 Motorized cycles
36 "A mouse!"
37 Gee preceders
39 Writer __ Hubbard
40 Tabula __ (clean slate)
44 Impersonated
46 Sample food
47 Stash away
48 Singer Skinnay
49 Service grp.
50 Peru natives
51 Like some Nolan Ryan performances
53 Culinary garnish
54 Mailed
57 Whirring sound
60 Not well
61 CBS logo
62 Treasure
63 Co., in Quebec

by Robert H. Wolfe

ACROSS

1 Humor response
5 Mass ending
9 "I've __ up to here!"
14 Pizzeria need
15 Great review
16 Martini extra
17 Margarita extra
18 George Peppard film of '66
20 Where the money goes
21 __ Antonio, TX
22 Concurrence
23 Plums' kin
25 Cotton thread
27 Plummet
29 "New" prefix
30 Collude in crime
34 Sign of a hit
36 Cosmetic
38 Football coach Don
39 Actress Del Rio
41 Hair dressings
43 Ease
44 Political football
46 __ Plaines, IL
47 Deciding factors
48 Compass pt.
49 Ribald
51 Knight workers
53 African capital
56 They should be respected
60 Tailor of song
62 A lot
63 Eastwood film of '71
65 Jean Stein bestseller
66 Steamed
67 Eye drop
68 Chances
69 Starchy veggie
70 Author Ferber
71 Wall St. org.

DOWN

1 Runs the show
2 Benefit
3 Streisand film of '69
4 Bullwinkle feature
5 They may be liberal
6 Taj __
7 Dark hours
8 Neighbor of 34 Down
9 Blackjacker's opponent
10 Pub potions
11 Thin coin
12 The typical Russian
13 Student's burden
19 Composer Schifrin
24 Rueful
26 Flows in slowly
28 "Annabel Lee" creator
30 "Gotcha!"
31 Lemmon/Matthau film of '81
32 Gen. Robt. __
33 Former Soviet news agency
34 Mt. Rushmore's home
35 Part
37 Taking advantage of
38 Fingerpainter's stroke
40 U.S. alliance
42 __ *Town*
45 Gets mad
48 "Adam had 'em" poet
50 Entrained
51 Snoop
52 Transparent wrap
54 H_2SO_4 and HCl
55 Plural pronoun
56 Computer command
57 One coin in the fountain?
58 "Godfrey Daniels!"
59 Feminine suffix
61 Role for Raquel
64 Eroded

55 MONSTERMEISTERS

by Wayne R. Williams

ACROSS

1 "Non più andrai," e.g.
5 Brown furs
11 "Gotcha!"
14 Remain undecided
15 Folkloric cave dwellers
16 San Francisco hill
17 Author of "The Colour Out of Space"
19 Collar
20 Worldwide workers' grp.
21 __ Downs (racetrack)
22 Alluring
23 Peace-loving
25 Broadway figure
28 Superlatively sugary
31 Price ceilings
34 Tuneful Travis
35 Polar region
36 USMC rank
39 Imperial Russian Ballet, today
41 Time remembered
42 Almighty, in Hebrew text
45 White Sea bay
48 Disarm a bull
49 Having a hissing sound
53 Gentle push
55 Flowering shrub
56 Deck officer: Abbr.
58 Buy new weapons
61 Rower's need
62 Nest-egg $$$
63 Author of *Watchers*
66 Greek cross
67 Toxic gas
68 On the briny
69 Pipe shape
70 Planting device
71 Actor Rip

DOWN

1 Garden pests
2 Do a farm job again
3 Smitten
4 Botheration
5 Author of *Cujo*
6 Trajectories
7 One of five in NYC
8 Camel kin
9 Mischievous creature
10 Mach topper
11 Author of *The Mummy*
12 Sham
13 Actress Dalton
18 Hearth goddess
22 Vague amount
24 Comparative ending
26 *The Hellbound Heart* author
27 Muscle spasm
29 "Star Wars" abbr.
30 New guys
32 Old salt
33 Healing waters
36 Frenzied
37 Fruity quaff
38 Author of *Shadows*
40 Sailors' spy grp.
43 Part of speech
44 Difficult, for a Cockney
46 Gadget
47 So. state
50 King in *The Tempest*
51 More cool
52 Jungle hunk
54 Wipe clean
56 Take the bait
57 Preacher Roberts
59 Author Bagnold
60 "Rule Britannia" composer
63 German article
64 Afore
65 Feedbag morsel

by Dean Niles

ACROSS

1 Whole bunch
5 Disney deer
10 Squabble
14 Tiny bit
15 Verdi selections
16 Tan-lotion ingredient
17 Lei land
18 Wash cycle
19 Elvis __ Presley
20 Nabokov novel
21 Diversion
23 Author Silverstein
25 Certain curves
26 Guiding light
29 Kerrigan's footwear
32 Bring toward fruition
33 The pokey
34 Rocker Reed
37 Office work
41 Whole bunch
42 Straw in the wind
43 Protection
44 PC operating system
46 The President, sometimes
47 Westminster __
50 *The __ of the Story* (Paul Harvey book)
51 Show prize
55 Maybe, maybe not
59 Michael or Susannah
60 "__-porridge hot"
61 Father
62 Rice drink
63 Composer Erik
64 Baking place
65 Gang ending
66 Different
67 Fishermen's needs

DOWN

1 Fool
2 Monetary advance
3 Needle case
4 Wooden wall lining
5 Unproductive
6 Spirit of *The Tempest*
7 Obey
8 Wild party
9 "Uh-huh"
10 Few and far between
11 The City of Light
12 Have __ to pick (complain)
13 Strong flavors
22 Not active: Abbr.
24 Work on the edge
26 Cry loudly
27 Cavern effect
28 Go __ (contend)
29 Markdowns
30 See 64 Across
31 __ carte
33 Kenyatta of Kenya
34 Corporate identifier
35 Emmy's cousin
36 Gorbachev's realm, once
38 Food fish
39 Charlotte and kin
40 Cast away
44 More compliant
45 Isr. neighbor
46 Surface appearance
47 Bottomless pit
48 Puff up
49 Delta of TV
50 Riveter of WWII
52 __ facto
53 Totally exhausted
54 Shower site
56 Lincoln's bill
57 Stew
58 Urges

57 SIT ON IT

by Shirley Soloway

ACROSS

1 Actress Ullmann
4 Former Surgeon General
8 Pitching ace Warren
13 Part to play
14 PBS science series
15 "... after they've seen __"
16 Object of devotion
17 "The __ Love"
18 Opening bars
19 Court order
22 Miles or Ferguson
23 Largest continent
24 __-mo replay
27 __ about
29 Ed of mystery
31 Ticked off
34 Evening working hours
37 In its present condition
39 Bud's sidekick
40 *Pretty Woman* star
41 Meeting conductor
46 Matched pieces
47 Actor Michael
48 Russian despot
50 Miner's discovery
51 Sonja Henie's birthplace
54 Move furtively
57 Informers
60 Outpouring
63 Pertaining to lyric poetry
64 Mr. Kringle
65 Famous fur merchant
66 Put on the market
67 Comical Kett
68 Nerds
69 Perry's penner
70 German article

DOWN

1 Sources of 50 Across
2 Massey of films
3 Fastening material
4 Smarts
5 Mrs. Chaplin
6 __ barrel (helpless)
7 Twosomes
8 Popeye's power source
9 Hyperventilate
10 Sculpture, for one
11 That girl
12 Prefix for "new"
13 Barbequed bone
20 Fictional Brinker
21 Points at the target
24 Cash keepers
25 Liquid measure, in London
26 Beginning
28 Exasperate
30 Tom Hanks film
31 Very large in scope
32 *My Name Is __ Lev*
33 Ms. Keaton
35 Negative conjunction
36 Surge of wind
38 Transgression
42 Some mob members
43 Mexican money
44 Small bone
45 Da __, Vietnam
49 Smelled bad
52 Untied
53 More mature
55 Main artery
56 Makes a muffler
57 Corner sign
58 Caplet, e.g.
59 Entitlement org.
60 Observed
61 Greek letter
62 24-hr. banking aid

58 DUTCH TREAT

by Bob Lubbers

ACROSS
1 Floral oil
6 Big bash
10 Ore source
14 Cook onions
15 In the sack
16 Over again
17 Metric weights, for short
18 Former Netherlands inlet
20 Pointless
22 Church officers
23 African antelope
25 Taj Mahal site
27 Sent a wire
28 Gave
33 Grounded bird
34 Novelist Anya
36 Went by burro
37 Physically fit
39 Incites anger
41 Cereal holder
42 Elapse
43 Anglers' awakeners
45 Modern recording syst.
46 Hearts of the matter
49 Dancing Chita
51 Courtroom recitation
52 Makes powdery
53 Flight segments
57 Editor's marks
58 Things to tilt at
61 __ *Majesty's Secret Service* ('69 film)
64 Pedestal percher
65 Verne's captain
66 __ ear and out the other
67 Kelly or Hackman
68 Has
69 Wanting

DOWN
1 "__ not what your country . . ."
2 Mai __ (cocktail)
3 Spring sprouters
4 Keyless
5 Used-car deals
6 Stare
7 __ Dhabi
8 Aloha gift
9 Poisonous snakes
10 Animal fat
11 11, in France
12 Forest forager
13 Maa belles?
19 Aqaba port
21 Consumer advocate Ralph
23 Glacial epoch
24 Ballroom dances
25 Do away with
26 *The Maids* playwright
29 Sphere
30 Wynken and Blynken's boat
31 __ *Scissorhands*
32 River features
35 Shangri-La setting
38 Center of a hurricane
40 Lint-grabbing material
44 Steak cut
47 Comedian Crosby
48 Bettors' mecca
50 River to the Loire
53 Canteen mouthful
54 Neap or spring
55 Unknown auth.
56 Sit in neutral
57 Mil. decorations
59 *Ben-Hur* author Wallace
60 K-O link
62 Wind up
63 *The Bridge of San Luis __*

59 BLOW ME DOWN!

by Fred Piscop

ACROSS

1 Slider, e.g.
6 Thom of shoedom
10 Designer Picone
14 Courtyards
15 Florence's river
16 Italian island resort
17 Coney Island coaster
19 School founded in 1440
20 Gram or decimal starter
21 Word form for "ear"
22 Wash basin
24 Vietnamese seaport
27 Retail transactions
28 Comic Chuck
31 Take five
33 In favor of
34 Conical abodes
37 "__ the ramparts . . ."
40 Boxer in a Dylan song
44 Last letter
45 Miniature mint
46 Drivers' org.
47 Former member of the UN
49 Mortar mate
51 Chief Justice, 1941-46
54 Most prudent
57 Marquee word
59 Martial-arts legend Bruce
60 The Beatles' "__ Love Her"

64 Way out
65 Chicago Bears great
68 "Have a __ day!"
69 Fed. agent
70 Composer Ned
71 Change for a five
72 Yemeni capital
73 Covered with white stuff

DOWN

1 Bike lane
2 Spillane's __ Jury
3 Dinosaur, for short
4 Noisy insect
5 "That ain't __!"
6 Island nation
7 Emulate Bing
8 Abby's twin
9 Mr. Coward
10 Otis invention
11 Like some statistics
12 Sun-dried brick
13 Verboten items
18 Hooks up
23 Silly person
25 Opposed to
26 Say "hi" to
28 Tach abbr.
29 Santa __, CA
30 Apple throwaway
32 Prison-wall jumpers
35 Noah's passengers
36 Business letter abbr.

38 Coup d'__
39 Not imaginary
41 Brings together again
42 Holes-in-one
43 Comic Charlotte
48 Prepare the table
50 Leave later
51 Office worker
52 Antidote target
53 In reserve
55 Edgar __ Poe
56 Actress Davis
58 Green __ and Ham
61 Cruel ruler
62 Took a card
63 God __ Co-Pilot
66 G.P. grp.
67 __ Gratia Artis

COLORFUL STATIONERY

by Harvey Estes

ACROSS

1 Church area
5 *Cabaret* singer
9 G-sharp's alias
14 Beethoven's birthplace
15 Eye part
16 Sister's girl
17 Bachelor's pride
19 Bride's follower
20 Sea life
21 Compass dir.
22 Goes on one's way
23 Denver clock setting: Abbr.
25 Rub a blade on stone
27 Circus swings
32 Boo-boo list
36 "__ Master's Voice"
37 Phone-book section
39 Follower of John
41 *Cheers* role
42 Beseech
43 Government reports
48 Poetic preposition
49 Shawl for a señor
50 Most cobra-infested
52 Truth stretcher
54 Racket
55 Produces 34 Down
58 __ in apple
61 "Last of the Red Hot __" (Sophie Tucker)
65 Sneeze sound
66 Schematic
68 Correct
69 Cosby show
70 *Beetle Bailey* barker
71 "Walk Away __"
72 Measure of medicine
73 Produce 34 Down

DOWN

1 Eban of Israel
2 Roper report
3 Fly in the ointment
4 Pitch a tent
5 Ad __ (wing it)
6 Wedge or niblick
7 National park in Utah
8 Out of whack
9 Belgian city
10 Tinderbox
11 Tilt
12 Etching liquid
13 Perfect diving scores
18 Author Ken
24 __-kung (Chinese city)
26 Use an ax
27 Goes soft
28 Nouveau __
29 Up and about
30 *Born Free* name
31 Hits open-handed
33 See eye to eye
34 Eye drops?
35 So far
38 Portentous sign
40 He's had a Rocky career
44 Part of a serial
45 Soup ingredient
46 Totally awesome
47 Cut corners
51 Straight
53 Like a mad dog
55 Boxer Max
56 Highest point
57 "__ in Rome . . ."
59 Too
60 Has an evening meal
62 Bit
63 Penny, often
64 Word on an octagon
67 Needle hole

61 HIGH STEPPIN'

by Shirley Soloway

ACROSS
1 Mold
6 FDR's pet
10 Kuwait native
14 Kid around with
15 Eddie or Richard
16 Ward of *Sisters*
17 Together (with)
18 Broadway light
19 Look over
20 Evades the issue
23 Takes one's leave
24 Finery
25 Pet tenders
29 Sandy substance
31 Possessing talent
32 Fire residue
33 Cereal grain
36 One isn't enough
41 Compass pt.
42 Roundish
43 Frozen desserts
44 Actress Meg
45 Without purpose
48 French farewell
51 As well
52 Completing easily
59 "Thanks __!"
60 Challenge
61 Courtyards
62 Nevada city
63 Concluded
64 Get to work
65 Actress Cannon
66 Majors and Marvin
67 Flies alone

DOWN
1 Mild argument
2 Luau entertainment
3 Surmounting
4 Toad abode
5 Hire
6 Real-estate markers
7 Tommie and James
8 Cambodia's neighbor
9 "Getting to Know You" singer
10 Classify
11 Happen again
12 __-Dale
13 Toss back and forth
21 Partner of neither
22 Singer Bonnie
25 Destiny
26 Abba of Israel
27 Actress Sommer
28 Poor grade
29 Obtained
30 Aussie jumper
32 Impresario Hurok
33 Fairy tale opener
34 Stone, Bronze and Iron
35 Pitch
37 Soviet spaceship
38 Hydroelectric agcy.
39 Pale-faced
40 Feel under the weather
44 Gymnast Mary Lou
45 Makes changes to
46 __ Kabibble
47 Swampy place
48 Oscar or Tony
49 Chicago mayor Richard
50 Massey of the movies
51 Match up
53 Adored one
54 Church area
55 Director Preminger
56 Russian range
57 Copter relative
58 Head warmers

by Dean Niles

ACROSS

1 Open one's big mouth
5 __ at (deride)
10 Biblical sufferer
13 Lord over
14 "Horrible" comics character
15 One of Hamlet's options
16 In a short time
17 Jane Curtin role
18 Hold back
19 38 Across' Oscar winner
22 1953 Alan Ladd western
23 Con job
24 Biological group
28 Not too swift
32 Letter writer's addenda: Abbr.
35 Russian range
37 Let up
38 Hollywood heavyweight
42 TV comic Bob
43 Church recess
44 Ruby or Sandra
45 Like some novels
47 Historic Crimean city
50 Slapstick projectiles
52 Intentional conflagration
56 Film directed by 38 Across
61 '60s musical
62 Relocation specialist
63 Celtic language
64 Chops down
65 Nitrogen compound
66 Root cause
67 Between, to Browning
68 Central points
69 Retton's scores

DOWN

1 Copper-zinc alloy
2 Out to __ (inattentive)
3 Islands hello
4 Actress Annette
5 Herring kin
6 Use the phone
7 Give the eye
8 County occasions
9 Painting on plaster
10 Louis and Frazier
11 Newspaper notice
12 Painter Shahn
15 Airplane stabilizer
20 Maiden-name preceder
21 Tag
25 *Sister Act* extra
26 Sky bear
27 Mawkish
29 Took advantage of
30 Desiccated
31 Boundary
32 "Hey, you!"
33 __-crossed (ill-fated)
34 __ Genesis (Nintendo rival)
36 Actress Hartman
39 Evening service
40 Moral value
41 Slippery one
46 Naval petty officer
48 Greek cross
49 Put a stop to
51 Replay effect
53 Wild time
54 Merlin or Ole
55 Craves
56 Hirsch sitcom
57 Sped
58 *Metamorphoses* poet
59 M. Descartes
60 CEO, often
61 Overdoer of a sort

63 OINK SPOTS

by Robert Herrig

ACROSS

1 Anna's adopted land
5 "Big" burger
8 Plummeted
12 Small land mass
13 Nasty habits
15 Surface size
16 Market patron of rhyme
19 Calendar column heading
20 Nuptial site
21 Knack
24 Tart-tasting
25 Family MDs
28 Italian instrument
30 Rogue
32 Strauss of jeans
33 Plumber's joints
36 Standish's stand-in
37 Ozarkian grunters
40 Better fit
41 Shirley Temple's first husband
42 Senior member
44 Sentra maker
46 In accordance with truth
48 Expert
49 __ + tissue = makeshift kazoo
52 Rope loops
53 *Zoo Story* playwright
54 Econ. calculation
55 Storied homebuilders
62 Rock musical
63 Result
64 Daredevil Knievel
65 Fire man?
66 Spud sprout
67 Depend

DOWN

1 Command to Beethoven
2 Sort of a suffix?
3 "The Greatest"
4 Entrances
5 Cambridge coll.
6 Take the role of
7 Casals' instrument
8 Cloudless
9 Little bit of work
10 Hose filler
11 Install carpeting
13 Port authority?
14 Delivery extra
17 Actress Anderson
18 Avoided one
21 "My mama done __ me ..."
22 Bitterly harsh
23 Ravel work
25 Kitchen wonders
26 Before the auction
27 Junior, for one
29 Goya patron
31 Heavy shoe
34 Fall behind
35 Lasting impression
38 Clairvoyant
39 Santa's alias
40 Trivia collection
43 Gov. Pataki's territory
45 __ *House* (Clavell epic)
47 Vanished
50 Potsdam possessive
51 Ms. Ross
53 Pertaining to planes
55 Article
56 Falstaff's pal
57 Periphery
58 Follower of 19 Across
59 I have shrunk?
60 Toothpaste type
61 Arch

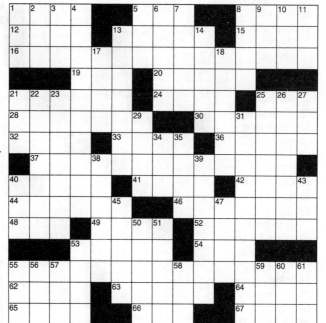

64 AYE-AYE

by Shirley Soloway

ACROSS

1 Nonsense
5 Skiers' transport
9 Asian desert
13 Art Deco artist
14 Former Attorney General Janet
15 Bodybuilder, perhaps
16 All over
17 Singer Anita
18 Prayer endings
19 Winter Olympics event
22 Aves.
23 Alias initials
24 Coffeemaker
25 Midwest Native Americans
31 Sign up
34 Dorothy's pet
35 __ Abner
36 Egg on
37 Animator Barbera's partner
39 Logical
40 Supply with weapons
41 __ Alto, CA
42 Stitch over again
43 Capital of Campania
47 Court divider
48 Short snooze
49 Skater Babilonia
52 Maui, for one
57 Turner and namesakes
58 Wise __ owl
59 __ time (never)
60 Pack away
61 Shade of green
62 Accessory for Salome
63 Take care of
64 Rude reply
65 Mars, to the Greeks

DOWN

1 Wampum units
2 "Ready __!"
3 Hearty entrees
4 Chopped down
5 Russian wagon
6 State of wild confusion
7 Job for a psych.
8 Rogers and Clark
9 Astrological sign
10 Portent
11 Loud sound
12 Election winners
15 Coiffure
20 Signal a cab
21 __ Kinte (*Roots* role)
25 Hip
26 "Let __ be said . . ."
27 Charged particle
28 Word of woe
29 Mid-evening
30 Did in
31 Actor Richard
32 Asta's mistress
33 Incline
37 Caribbean nation
38 Ring champ
39 Baltic or Bering
41 Make happy
42 Tears
44 Ahead
45 Historical records
46 Frankie and Cleo
49 Spud
50 Warbucks' charge
51 Role models
52 Abhor
53 In a while
54 Fleming and Paisley
55 Europe's neighbor
56 Volcanic flow
57 Mil. vehicle

65 ON THE DIAL

by Sally R. Stein

ACROSS

1 Tree branch
5 Showed fear
10 "Okey-__!"
14 Where Laos is
15 "__ a stinker?"
16 Andy's pal
17 Misfortunes
18 Sports data
19 Runners of song
20 Superman's dressing room
23 Bearing
24 Coffee vessel
25 Goes along
28 Compass point, in Paris
30 Mail-order regulators: Abbr.
33 Breakfast food
34 Bull or Bullwinkle
35 Seatless state, initially
36 Wheeler-dealer
40 Tune from *A Chorus Line*
41 Claude of *Casablanca*
42 Be overfond
43 QB's scores
44 Mean monster
45 Bowler's prize
47 Abby's sister
48 Burn a bit
49 Digital exercise book?
56 Mardi __
57 Jeweled headband
58 Party cheese
59 Greek liqueur
60 Tube preceder
61 Singular
62 Road Runner's syllable
63 Slide downhill
64 Water jug

DOWN

1 Café au __
2 South Seas site
3 Steel factory
4 Last place, figuratively
5 Military bands?
6 Discover, as an idea
7 __ uproar
8 Minimizing suffix
9 Pay out
10 Pythias' pal
11 Forget to include
12 Former mayor of New York
13 180 degrees from WNW
21 Missile for Soupy Sales
22 Waiter's request
25 Monastery man
26 Monotony
27 Goes ape
28 Not a soul
29 Klutz's remark
30 Lens setting
31 Promise to marry
32 Nutty professor Irwin __
34 Former Israeli prime minister
37 Literary twist
38 Rife with charisma
39 Darn cute
45 Ruin someone's plans
46 Culpability
47 Old-time storyteller
48 Apple trash
49 Multiple-choice answer
50 Morning weather
51 Floor covering, for short
52 Turner around Hollywood
53 Shoot up
54 __ *kleine Nachtmusik*
55 Future examiner
56 Sea dog

by Shirley Soloway

ACROSS

1 Bread unit
5 Lord's mate
9 John or Don
14 Swedish pop group
15 The Emerald Isle
16 Rocker David
17 Christmas carol
18 Fusses
19 1984 Kentucky Derby winner
20 The farmer's milieu
21 Short snooze
22 Submerged, as a doughnut
23 Lyric poem
25 Car part
27 Had a yen for
30 Surpass
31 Sanctuary
32 Lockhart of *Lassie*
33 Ski-lift feature
37 Baker's aide
38 Dove shelters
39 Sharpen
40 Peter of the piano
41 Wedding words
42 Hammer parts
43 "__ I can help it!"
45 Have second thoughts
46 Wigwams
48 Corn serving
49 Partial
50 Doctrine
52 Brewer's oven
56 Adjust
57 *The African Queen* writer
58 Arm bone
59 __ Rogers St. Johns
60 Herring
61 Lunchtime for some
62 Feudal workers
63 Give it __
64 Names, as a knight

DOWN

1 Touch down
2 Woodwind instrument
3 Cain's brother
4 Be excessively eager
5 Stood (against)
6 Verdi work
7 Disappears
8 Word of agreement
9 Ridiculous
10 Completely
11 Up and about
12 Bannister or Ryun
13 Burpee offering
22 Sees socially
24 Lion's lair
26 Melodies
27 Beard locale
28 Competition
29 State with conviction
32 Foster of *Maverick*
34 Certain South African
35 Bancroft or Boleyn
36 Musical pause
38 Referred to
42 Soup veggie
44 6 Down and others
45 Cure
46 Spanish mark
47 Refrige-raider
49 Sheep sounds
51 Seal in the juices
53 Baseball manager Felipe
54 Snooty one
55 Takes the sun
57 Cool __ cucumber

67 YOUR HIT PARADE

by Bob Lubbers

ACROSS

1 Aunts: Sp.
5 Entice
9 After-shower wraps
14 Author Rice
15 Vicinity
16 Parriers' needs
17 Needle
19 Snitches (on)
20 Captivate
21 Holy one
23 Not as much
26 West Point freshmen
29 "Who's on first?" asker
33 Draw a new line
34 Tense, slangily
35 Had a pain
37 Crow call
38 Very dry
39 Polynesian carvings
40 __ terrier
41 Luau dip
42 Wove a chair seat
43 1040 submitter
44 Evelyn of *The Wolf Man*
46 Longing ones
48 Country singer Jim
49 Perry's creator
50 Tag, bridge, etc.
52 __ de corps
57 Word form for "red"
59 Joke ending
62 Greek physician
63 Estrada or Satie
64 Shoppe descriptor
65 Libyan gulf
66 Eugene V. __
67 Unskilled laborer

DOWN

1 Recording medium
2 Privy to
3 Singer Paul
4 Appear to be
5 Partner of Hardy
6 Coffee maker
7 Stephen of *Angie*
8 Diner sign
9 Redid the bathroom, perhaps
10 First game of a series
11 Clasp of a sort
12 Wriggly fish
13 Draft grp.
18 Former House Speaker
22 After: Fr.
24 Done in
25 Kind of salmon
27 Ionospheric region
28 Underground ducts
29 One of the Magi
30 Nine-__ (emergency number)
31 Succeed
32 Mao __-tung
36 Escapee, maybe
39 Cup, in Calais
40 Envy or sloth, e.g.
42 Amati's hometown
43 Sassy
45 Tax cheat, perhaps
47 Smart __ (wise guys)
51 Went too fast
53 Drip sound
54 Steam up
55 __-European
56 College freshman, usually
57 Football linemen: Abbr.
58 "Bali __"
60 Ending for press
61 Penpoint

68 INITIAL REACTION

by Ray Smith

ACROSS

1 *I Remember* __
5 Toddlers
10 Does sums
14 Desertlike
15 "__ of robins"
16 Dull sound
17 Short sprint
18 Tobacco manufacturer
20 Never-captured hijacker
22 Turner and Cantrell
23 Not van. or straw.
24 Tendon
25 Campaign '64 letters
28 Pre-cable need
30 Cincinnati baseballer
33 Commands
35 Make a hole
36 Toy-block brand
37 Costume jewelry
38 Pepper or York: Abbr.
39 Dance that "takes two"
40 Perón and Gabor
41 Actor's prompt
42 Relief
43 Our sun
44 Stogie
46 USNA grad
47 Wight and Capri
49 Learning method
51 Put in a chip
52 Former Giants quarterback
56 Tire magnate
58 Signal (a cab)
59 Hurler Hershiser
60 Fruit for cider or sauce
61 Miss Fitzgerald
62 Put to sleep?
63 *The Sun Also* __
64 Curb

DOWN

1 Road-safety org.
2 Saudi, for one
3 Catchall abbr.
4 Kind of committee
5 Florida game fish
6 Inoculate
7 Deborah or Jean
8 Language suffix
9 Teasing, as hair
10 Make up (for)
11 *Sons and Lovers* author
12 Lemons
13 '60s campus grp.
19 *Peter Pan* dog
21 Busy airport
24 Testy state
25 Easy strides
26 Theater cheer
27 Holden Caulfield's creator
29 Gardening tool
31 Prod
32 Portals
34 ALF et al.
36 Fond du __, WI
38 Brings to court
39 __-frutti ice cream
41 Aged yellow cheese
42 Comforts
44 Role for Liz
45 Seer
48 Fur wrap
50 Anesthetic
51 Bushy hairdo
52 Kennel sounds
53 Yarn
54 "__ Marlene" (WWI song)
55 Enthusiasm
56 Newhart or Cousy
57 Troy, NY coll.

69 DISNEY WORLD

by S.N.

ACROSS

1 Impassive
6 G.P.'s grp.
9 Big shot
14 *Your Show of Shows* host
16 Political event
17 Disney's first sound cartoon: 1928
19 The "white" in Great White Way
20 Curved letter
21 Variety show VIPs
24 Joplin creation
25 Deep black
26 Mid.
29 This __ (choice words)
31 Beat walker
32 Kingston, e.g.
33 Ricochet
34 Temporary
36 Best Song Oscar recipient: 1947
38 Marginalia
39 "Ditto!"
41 Donna or Robert
42 Shaving-cream type
43 Dressy hat
44 Fed. collectors
45 Driller's deg.
46 Noticed
47 Ward healers?
48 Large lake
49 Epithet for Earl Hines
51 With *The*, TV series: 1955-59
58 Foul-smelling
59 Rake over the coals

60 Drudges
61 Penultimate letter
62 Like knives

DOWN

1 Draft org.
2 __ for tat
3 Shelley opus
4 "__ See Clearly Now"
5 Film-crew member
6 "With __ in My Heart"
7 Lea sounds
8 Illustration
9 Watch place for many
10 Haarlem painter
11 Plumber's piece

12 Yalie
13 Soap ingredient
15 PT's opposite number
18 "__ more, my lady . . ."
21 Summer shoe, for short
22 More wacko
23 Walks broadly
25 Steinbeck family
26 Disney, vis-á-vis 17 Across
27 Small-time
28 Decay
30 Trusted
31 Angler's need
32 __ over (saw through difficulty)
34 French noodles?
35 *West Side Story* tune

37 __ *Afternoon* (Pacino film)
38 __ Lanka
40 W. Hemisphere alliance
43 Dom DeLuise movie of '80
45 Exploits
46 Pasta topping
48 Wiener covering
49 Arch
50 Sulfuric or carbolic
51 Work by Mercator
52 Cola cooler
53 __-Magnon
54 Kittenish remark
55 Fall behind
56 Western Indian
57 Murphy, for one

ACROSS

1 Quite bright
6 Commercial creator
11 Wager
14 Thespian
15 Idaho's capital
16 Midwest Indian
17 Western desperado
19 Government agcy.
20 "Michael, Row Your Boat __"
21 From a distance
22 Gregorian singers
25 Heathens
27 Glove insert
28 Spot for a boutonniere
29 Coffeepot
30 Ozzie and Harriet
34 __ Yeller
37 Three: Pref.
38 Superimpose
39 Spelling contest
40 Give the __ (ogle)
41 Madmen
42 "__ Got a Crush on You"
43 Forebodings
45 Toboggan
46 Hears (of)
48 Peter and Paul
52 Vessels
53 Topnotch
54 Nev. neighbor
55 He rode with Jesse James
60 Compass dir.
61 Solo

62 Frightening
63 Susan of L.A. Law
64 Preclude
65 Marsh plant

DOWN

1 Day of rest: Abbr.
2 Sprint competitor
3 Part of NATO
4 Chanson de __
5 Assignation
6 Loathe
7 Movers and shakers
8 Newsman Wallace
9 "__ was saying . . ."

10 Actor Beatty
11 Wild West Show organizer
12 __ Frome
13 Rips
18 Useful article
21 Ripen
22 Skydiver's need, for short
23 Ike's predecessor
24 Western markswoman
25 Lose control
26 Church areas
28 Singer Falana
30 "__ allowed" (ladies only)
31 Cowgirl Dale
32 Camera part
33 __ Lanka

35 River embankment
36 Property titles
44 The Ghost and __ Muir
45 Point of view
46 Spiked, as punch
47 Wipe out
48 Stadium
49 He treats
50 Meter preceder
51 Children's-book pseudonym
53 Clump
55 Scoundrel
56 Bullfight cheer
57 Wander
58 Unit of work
59 Deli bread

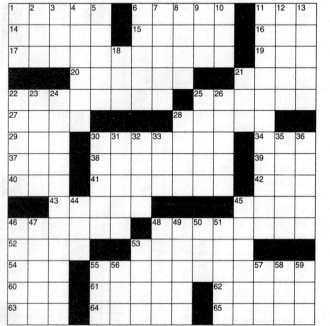

71 WASH DAY

by Dean Niles

ACROSS

1 Some saxes
6 Futures exchange, for short
10 Word of relief
14 Deception
15 Unexciting
16 Past the deadline
17 Certain line segments
18 He loved an Irish Rose
19 Pilaster
20 __ kind (unique)
22 Ornamental flower
24 One's salary, to an accountant
26 Vitamin stats.
27 Tied up
29 __ Cruces, NM
30 Voice origin
34 __ Kabibble
35 "For shame!"
36 Plead
37 Poet's eternity
38 "Agnus __"
39 Salt's response
40 Oscar-winning composer Francis __
41 Span. lady
42 Work unit
43 Mil. branch
44 Bustle
45 Green climber
46 Top type
48 Gold source
49 Grant and Madigan
50 Litigate against
51 North African
53 Send along
57 Most definite
60 Desire
61 It's easy
63 Climbing vine
64 Former Atlanta arena
65 Author Godwin
66 Stevedore, e.g.
67 Dick and Jane's dog
68 __ account
69 More wily

DOWN

1 Frizzy top
2 Director David
3 Blondie song
4 Spicy, in a way
5 Unyielding
6 Grad. degree
7 Pushes aside
8 Train track
9 Sidelines yellers
10 2-D
11 It's given in marriage
12 Suffix for kitchen
13 Put on
21 Encouraging words
23 Slow tempo
25 Of a hard wood
27 Basinlike fixture
28 Those who partake
31 Song of '65
32 Brash
33 Medical photos
35 Ford model
36 Racket
47 "__ Romantic?"
48 Garner
49 Auto appendage
52 Chicago cagers
53 Pairs
54 Slanting surface
55 __ Domini
56 __ uproar
58 Snicker-__
59 Region: Abbr.
62 Arafat grp.

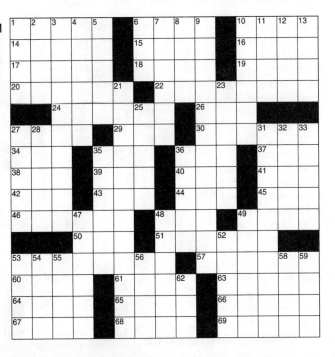

72 BE A DEER

by Shirley Soloway

ACROSS

1 Rum cakes
6 Lettuce relative
10 A long way off
14 Make happy
15 Nutritional need
16 Pasternak heroine
17 "He's somebody __ problem . . ." (L. Hart lyric)
18 "Bye!"
19 Do the backstroke
20 Shift blame
23 Short snooze
24 "When I Take My Sugar __"
25 British weapons
27 Smart
30 Madrid missus
33 Crack pilot
36 Jamie of *M*A*S*H*
38 At no time
39 Linden or Holbrook
40 "Get lost!"
42 N.Y. zone in August
43 Leg joint
45 Simplicity
46 Rogers or Clark
47 Command
49 John __ Garner
52 Cowboy flick
54 Things to be done
57 Comedian Erwin
59 Prenuptial get-togethers
63 Salad fish
65 "__ Clock Jump"
66 Capable
67 Remnants
68 Wimpy one
69 Fur-bearing swimmer
70 Intertwine
71 Gets the point
72 Jury members

DOWN

1 Electronic sound
2 __ sea (confused)
3 Opera singer
4 Bikini events
5 Six-line verse
6 Franklin's flyer
7 Part of UAR
8 Water lily
9 Passes, as a bill
10 Hirt and Pacino
11 Dotes on
12 Diva's solo
13 Incline
21 Israeli metropolis
22 New Hampshire city
26 Map dir.
28 Identify
29 React to a bad joke
31 Make over
32 Affected
33 Moby Dick captain
34 Sugar source
35 Norwegian canines
37 Madame __ (Signoret film)
40 Sleeveless jackets
41 "I __ Letter to My Love"
44 Actress Thompson
48 Wyoming range
50 Drive-in employee
51 House and grounds
53 Hindu queen
55 Kunta __ of *Roots*
56 Passover dinner
57 Flower holder
58 Melody
60 Richard of *Primal Fear*
61 Pea containers
62 Damascus citizens: Abbr.
64 Cigar end

73 SHIP SHAPE

by Richard Silvestri

ACROSS

1 Gangplank, e.g.
5 Lazarus and Thompson
10 Expended
14 Brainstorm
15 Press-release addressees
16 Hang around
17 Censorship of a sort
19 Possess
20 Lode stuff
21 Let down
23 Doing an impression
26 Echo, for short
27 Home shopping network?
28 Multi-faced one of film
30 Distribute
33 Yukon, for one: Abbr.
34 Banish
36 Tire filler
37 Try a contest
39 Moose kin
40 Start a set
42 I.D. info
43 Less difficult
46 "Et tu" time
47 Consolidates
49 Pinkerton's logo
50 Five from New Jersey
51 Gave a bash
53 Impolite looks
55 Plunderers
57 Terse prez
58 Be next to
59 Violin virtuoso
65 Teddy's mom
66 Closely compacted
67 Surface extent
68 Enthusiastic
69 Berlin's "The Song Is __"
70 Coddle

DOWN

1 Barbecued bit
2 Hoo-ha
3 Sound of a Siamese
4 Digs for a beatnik
5 Stepped forth
6 "A __ bagatelle!"
7 Half of MMMII
8 Bridal path
9 Russian Tea Room server
10 Theater group
11 Rooming-house VIP
12 Roof edge
13 Prepared Easter eggs
18 *The Ghost of Frankenstein* name
22 Nathanael and Rebecca
23 Get even for
24 Prime-rib neighbor
25 About
26 Made a response
27 First-stringers
29 Two-finger signs
31 Holds one's attention
32 Hank of hair
35 __-doke
38 Teammate of Campanella
41 __ *kleine Nachtmusik*
44 Riding a horse
45 Tightened the shoestrings
48 Acquired
52 German city
54 High rails
55 Good clean fun
56 Reed instrument
57 Job for Mason
60 &
61 Boxtop piece
62 Diamond stat.
63 Gray soldier
64 Negative vote

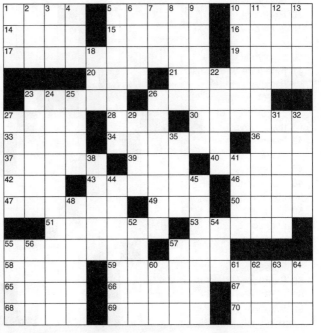

BODY WORK

by Shirley Soloway

ACROSS

1 Cadabra preceder
5 Suffix for special or final
8 Imitation
12 Runs in neutral
13 Not pro
14 Architect Saarinen
15 Harmonica
17 Treats leather
18 Vicinity
19 Laundry additive
21 On the __ (exactly)
22 Progression
24 Not moving
26 Cleo or Frankie
29 Go bad
31 Brit. fliers
34 Tall grasses
36 Reno or Leigh
38 Jean of *Arsenic and Old Lace*
40 Muslim title
41 Final Greek letter
42 XLIX sqvared?
43 "... emblem of the __ love"
45 Yanks' Boston rivals
46 "__ evil ..."
48 Equestrian's controls
50 Unclear
52 Like some modern music
56 Coach Parseghian
58 Exertion
61 FDR's dog
62 Scrabble piece
64 Stevie Wonder oldie
66 Musical composition
67 Eight: Pref.
68 Change for a ten
69 Chick's sound
70 Charlotte of TV
71 Astute

DOWN

1 Worship
2 Sadder
3 Not wholesale
4 Cigar residue
5 Swenson of *Benson*
6 Night-sky sights
7 Dyes: Poet.
8 Tennis match unit
9 Front-page screamers
10 Florence's river
11 Largest amount
12 "__ corny as Kansas ..."
13 Museum offering
16 Davis of *Evening Shade*
20 Swinging nightspot
23 Jewelry items
25 Sandy soil
27 Actress Patricia
28 Writer __ Rice Burroughs
30 Kids' block brand
31 St. Louis footballer
32 Navy V.I.P.s
33 Apparent worth
35 Rational
37 April 15 concern
39 Brainstorm
44 Sawyer or Ladd
47 Looking to obtain
49 Easy mark
51 Writer Jong
53 Uninformed
54 Of the Tyrol
55 Gaelic girl
56 Over
57 Ready to eat
59 Poker entry fee
60 "__ to Rio" (Peter Allen song)
63 Clairvoyant's talent: Abbr.
65 Former D.C. stadium

by Dean Niles

ACROSS

1 Popular '70s hairdo
5 Comics Viking
10 Unappetizing stuff
14 High wind
15 Last of a series
16 Casino city
17 Rowdy group
20 Sectors
21 Perfect grade
22 Civil War monogram
25 Debussy's sea
26 Highest
30 Washington's Kennedy __
32 Dad's boys
33 Colorado Native American
34 __ Thompson (Maugham character)
35 Ike's ex
36 Footnote phrase
37 Group members
40 Hem in
41 Clears
42 Best man's offering
44 Poet's contraction
45 Poet's tributes
46 Grass variety
47 Stuck
49 Sleeve filler
50 Ecol. org.
51 "__ Day Will Come"
52 Hardly right
54 Group's forte
61 Rani's garment
62 City near Gainesville
63 Pennsylvania port
64 Paired
65 Gallo products
66 Old horses

DOWN

1 Preston or Pepper: Abbr.
2 "Gotcha!"
3 Dark malt
4 Jazzman Stan
5 Little Jack __
6 Turkish title
7 The Bee __
8 Cabinet lawyers: Abbr.
9 Clear-thinking
10 Bride's mate
11 Without a __ to stand on
12 Impersonal pronoun
13 Batt. terminal
18 Family prep. course
19 Klutz's cry
22 Dosage amts.
23 More sleazy
24 Pyrenees nation
26 Theater honors
27 Beat Andretti, e.g.
28 Waits for Santa, perhaps
29 __ Aviv
31 Even-steven
32 Some sediments
35 Cornered
36 Love god
38 Surf phenomenon
39 Music marking
40 Procured
43 Pekoe or Earl Grey, e.g.
45 Magnum __ (masterpiece)
46 Uproar
48 Visit unexpectedly
49 Foot-leg link
52 See 60 Down
53 Govt. agents
54 JFK arrival
55 __ & Order
56 Jackie's second
57 Here, in Toulouse
58 Distinct period
59 Use a shovel
60 With 52 Down, Sammy Davis Jr. autobiography

ACROSS

1 Beer ingredient
5 Dieter's concern
10 Ax stroke
14 Mr. Nastase
15 "Live Free __" (NH motto)
16 Musical sample
17 Pigeonhole
19 Actor James
20 Bain or Hilton
21 Wood strip
23 Like the desert
24 European capital
26 Get ready to play golf
28 Doesn't get it, in a sense
32 More reckless
35 French friend
36 Winter precipitation
37 Mrs. Helmsley
38 Penny
40 Bore a hole
43 Close-fitting
44 __ the Horrible (comics Viking)
46 Fruit-filled desserts
48 Poetic preposition
49 Sign up
51 Gung-ho
53 Pixies
55 Valhalla resident
56 Ump kin
58 Special-interest orgs.
60 Prescribes
64 Allies' opponent
66 Ad creator
68 Thurber's The __ Animal
69 Labor group
70 Coup d'__
71 Church outcry
72 Sean and Arthur
73 Koran chapter

DOWN

1 Var. topics
2 Sax type
3 Legal claim
4 Overwhelming fear
5 Forest
6 Actor Carney
7 Pastoral poem
8 Nurse, as a drink
9 Fluctuate
10 Atlanta health agcy.
11 Walkman part
12 Mr. Sharif
13 Small horse
18 Relieves
22 Mend
25 Stink
27 Exploits for gain
28 Papier-__
29 Words of clarification
30 One way to march
31 Filch
33 Accustom
34 Vented one's spleen
39 End piece
41 Oilcloth, in Britain
42 Disappointments
45 Invitation letters
47 Bake eggs
50 China piece
52 Lingerie
54 British biscuit
56 "__ Lama Ding Dong"
57 Midterm, e.g.
59 Whirl around
61 "__, Brute?"
62 Bring up
63 Mlle. in Madrid
65 E.M. Kennedy's title
67 At that place

77 COLOR TELEVISION

by Harvey Estes

ACROSS

1 Life sketch
4 Jazz phrase
8 Bullets, for short
12 Sea birds
13 Walk __ (be elated)
15 Tail end
16 Gemini org.
17 "Be quiet!"
18 Is human?
19 '60s crime show
22 Show host
23 Word of cheer?
24 Gymnast Comaneci
26 Inform
27 Weed chopper
29 Words of surprise
31 Travelers' stop
32 "It" game
33 San Diego attraction
34 Editor's direction
35 '70s police show
39 Heart of the matter
40 Conclusion
41 Fall mo.
42 Singer Shannon
43 Salt Lake City setting: Abbr.
44 "Either he goes __ go!"
45 Friend of de Gaulle
48 Some circus performers
50 Actor Charleston
52 Agnew's nattering one
54 '80s sitcom
57 Puff-of-smoke sound

58 Pakistan neighbor
59 Allie's ally
60 Catch sight of
61 Takes it easy
62 Garden spot
63 Culp/Cosby program
64 Red mark
65 Beatty of *Deliverance*

DOWN

1 Hindu deity
2 Bug
3 Orange type
4 Got up
5 Not out there
6 Beasts in the flora
7 End of the line
8 The MCI Center, for one
9 Burgess of *Rocky*
10 Strict disciplinarian
11 Hosp. theaters
12 Computer key
14 Greek letter
20 Betty Ford Clinic work
21 Workers in 11 Down
25 Picnic pest
28 Stares at
30 Integrity
32 Singer Ritter
33 Last letter in London
34 An NCO
35 Where Tarzan swings

36 '50s toy
37 Up to this point
38 Cake cover
39 S&L concerns
43 Food-flavor enhancer: Abbr.
44 Big name in drama
45 Rub raw
46 Shed feathers
47 *Hedda Gabler* writer
49 Grove of baseball
51 Discombobulate
53 Conrad of verse
55 Black gold
56 Cartoonist Thomas
57 Pressure meas.

STORMY WEATHER

by Shirley Soloway

ACROSS

1 Offer a chair to
5 __ Major (Great Bear)
9 Greek letters
14 Wheel support
15 Tailor's line
16 Repent
17 Sounds from a comedy club
20 Land or sea follower
21 Nile snake
22 Consume
23 Robert Mitchum miniseries
28 Durango direction
29 Slangy denial
30 Health resort
33 Spring beauty
36 Taken-back purchases
40 Hi and bye?
44 Calm, as fears
45 The Elephant Boy
46 Mystery writer Josephine
47 Scottish denial
49 Concerned with
52 Summer night sights
58 __ capita
59 Pull a scam
60 __ Grows in Brooklyn
62 Car make
67 Belief
68 Broadway light
69 "__ Old Cowhand"
70 Bob of *Full House*

71 Sp. miss
72 Oscar __ Renta

DOWN

1 Droops
2 Precise
3 God of Islam
4 Indian tent
5 GI aid org.
6 Ring ump
7 Dinner course
8 Gather together
9 Groceries holder
10 Archaic verb ending
11 "When I Take My Sugar __"
12 Lend __ (listen)
13 Spanish artist
18 Plies a needle
19 Atop
24 "Put __ writing"
25 School outcasts
26 Cab cost
27 Sound of relief
30 __ Na Na
31 Buddy
32 Feel sick
34 __ *Man Answers* ('62 film)
35 Polio pioneer
37 Housecat, e.g.
38 Bullring cheer
39 Wily
41 Singer k.d. __
42 Indian nanny
43 Ladder step

48 Engrave
50 Ski lift
51 Offer more money
52 Martin Arrowsmith's wife
53 Not perf., as clothing
54 Verbs' subjects
55 __ *Sanctum*
56 Soot
57 Ecological adjective
58 Promoted pvts.
61 Author Ferber
63 '50s pres.
64 Little one
65 Period
66 Queen of Spain

79 YANKEE DOODLES

by Richard Silvestri

ACROSS

1 Echelon
5 Jefferson's belief
10 Big chunk
14 "This one's __!"
15 "Moldy" tune
16 Flag holder
17 Yankee Hall-of-Famer
19 Serenader's instrument
20 What enemies have lost?
21 Ring around the collar?
22 Dr. Frankenstein's assistant
23 In a snit
25 Outstanding
27 Corporate cow
29 Restraint
32 Stephen and William of Hollywood
35 Darth __
37 Fink
38 *Xanadu* group
39 Western scenery
40 "__ Got a Crush on You"
41 Silly Putty container
42 A bit more normal
43 Racing sleds
45 Hem maker
47 Take hold
49 "__ Ha'i"
50 $$$
54 Mass conclusion
56 Architectural deg.
59 Sun circler
60 High in alcohol
61 Yankee Hall-of-Famer
63 Zoning unit
64 San Antonio landmark
65 Differently
66 Minimal wampum
67 David's weapon
68 Report-card woes

DOWN

1 Burgs
2 __ water (trouble-bound)
3 Author Zola
4 Hauled again
5 Senior members
6 Subordinate Claus?
7 Admiree
8 Kingly address
9 Gets both sides together
10 First-aid item
11 Yankee Hall-of-Famer
12 Sort of sax
13 "The amber nectar"
18 What Pandora released
24 Specified
26 "__ the ramparts . . ."
28 Unburdens
30 Icicle locale
31 AAA selections
32 Exemplar of redness
33 Ms. Korbut
34 Yankee Hall-of-Famer
36 Challenged
39 Mexican music makers
42 The sun's name
43 Actress Palmer
44 Took sneakers off
46 Splashed down
48 Numero uno
51 Spat's spot
52 Singer Della
53 Eye infections
54 Gregory Peck's *Moby Dick* role
55 Anti-mugger weapon
57 Pervade
58 Jai __
62 K-O interior

by Shirley Soloway

ACROSS

1 Days gone by
5 Arizona river
9 Scent sensors
14 Man __ (racehorse)
15 Eden resident
16 Patriot Allen
17 Thompson of *Family*
18 Gaucho's weapon
19 Video-game name
20 Pathfinder
23 "Spring forward" time: Abbr.
24 Small sofa
25 First month, in Madrid
27 Approximately
30 Fishes with a net
33 Squelched
37 Landing place
39 Wading bird
40 "Holy cow!"
41 French director Louis
42 Classify
43 Tim of *Frank's Place*
44 Unit
45 Male and female
46 Composer Harold et al.
48 Lady of Spain
50 Welcome
52 Blake or Plummer
57 Lawyers' org.
59 List of accomplishments
62 Word before larceny or point
64 Burn
65 Yuletide buy
66 Eydie's mate
67 Casino game
68 Racetrack shape
69 Let up
70 Goulash
71 Baking apple

DOWN

1 Sends by mail
2 Cognizant
3 Mubarak's predecessor
4 Characteristic
5 Tongue wagger
6 Object of worship
7 Singing sounds
8 Stun
9 More reachable
10 Hall-of-Famer Mel
11 Spar solo
12 Corn servings
13 Foul mood
21 Writer Uris
22 __ nous (confidentially)
26 Lift up
28 Mild disagreement
29 Lubricated
31 Money in Milan
32 Overseas planes
33 Medical fluids
34 Teen follower
35 Football-party sites
36 More unusual
38 Seaman's saint
41 Penny-pincher
45 Identical
47 Retained after expenses
49 Not wide
51 Fasteners
53 Thespian
54 Vibes player Red
55 Sleep experience
56 Fred Astaire's sister
57 Church space
58 Letter after alpha
60 Newsman Huntley
61 Role for Welles
63 "__ Got Sixpence"

81 AS EASY AS...

by Fred Piscop

ACROSS
1 Castle protection
5 Chinchilla, e.g.
8 Country singer Charley
13 Chan's comment
14 Norwegian monarch
16 Sieved potatoes
17 ABC
20 Short vocal solo
21 Diplomats' quest
22 Kind of 26 Across
23 Had on
24 Prompter's lead-in
26 Fisherman
31 Former Sinclair competitor
35 Vaughn role
37 Duffer's shot
38 PIE
41 Lama land
42 Author Ephron
43 Sufficiently cooked
44 Lucky charm
46 Brewer's need
48 Actress Skye
50 Errand runner
55 Write scores
59 Bring in
60 1-2-3
62 Nine-headed serpent
63 Pâté de __ gras
64 Defeat
65 Lamb product

66 Draft agcy.
67 Sp. women

DOWN
1 Goya subjects
2 Chicago airport
3 Computer-code abbr.
4 Straphanger's purchase
5 Recliner part
6 Forearm bone
7 Spitfire flyers
8 Make-believe
9 Shine's partner
10 Computer-screen symbol
11 Fender bender

12 Leading __ (vanguard)
15 Pooch's name
18 Editor's mark
19 Actress Miles
23 Mat word
25 Beef cut
27 Tickled pink
28 Suction starter
29 Friedman's subj.
30 Actor Auberjonois
31 "¿Cómo __ usted?"
32 Singer Whitman
33 Star of India
34 German auto
36 Gumbo veggie
39 Big name in pianos

40 Game fish
45 Frat-party wear
47 Blue shade
49 Soft ball
51 Amorphous masses
52 Cut obliquely
53 California city
54 Fits together
55 Tennis great Arthur
56 Rogers and Acuff
57 Backwoods P.O. routes
58 Razor brand
59 Slugger's stats.
61 Dawn goddess

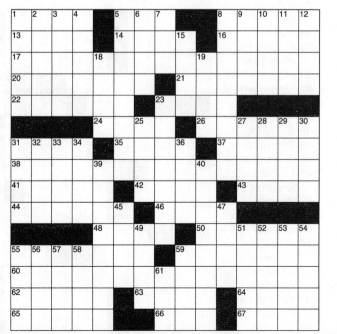

82 WISE WORDS

by Ann Seidel

ACROSS

1 Latin abbr.
5 Delhi's land
10 Strip of concrete
14 Actress Turner
15 Broadway lights
16 Lay concrete
17 Crafts' partner
18 Inspiration
20 Band leader
22 Motionless
23 Have debts
24 Carried
27 Words from experience
31 __ Dog (Terhune tale)
35 Embellish
36 "__ a man with seven wives"
37 K-6 school, for short
38 Auto
39 Brought the meeting to order
42 "Egg" word form
43 Recognized
45 El __, TX
46 Encounter
48 Jerk's offering
49 Corner that's less than 90 degrees
51 Throat problem
53 Steelers' org.
54 Artistic judgment
57 Of ancient Mexicans
61 What insiders bet with
65 __ mater

66 French girlfriend
67 Morning sound
68 Dines
69 Rock and __
70 Lake craft
71 "For __ jolly good fellow"

DOWN

1 Veteran actor Jack
2 O'Haras' residence
3 Pay to play
4 Cowboy, often
5 Not acquired
6 Evil emperor
7 "__ make myself clear?"
8 Gerund suffix
9 Cigar residue
10 "Do not fold, __, or mutilate"
11 Put on cargo
12 Swear
13 Patrol area
19 Overtime situation
21 Plucked sound
24 Proctor's call
25 Spotted wildcat
26 Head: Fr.
27 Baseball bases
28 A Bell for ___
29 Pierced, in a way
30 Lively, in music
32 "Take Me __"
33 Flavor eggs
34 Nitrogen compound
40 On __ with (equal to)

41 Kind of beer
44 Squanderer
47 Let loose
50 Digestive protein
52 Vietnamese New Year
54 Nicholas or Alexander
55 Bombs and bullets
56 Glide along
57 Dynamic beginning
58 Inkling
59 Fuse units
60 Gemini org.
62 PC alternative
63 Pay or scram ending
64 A Bobbsey

....

by Dean Niles

ACROSS

1 Photo holder
6 Bric-a-__
10 High-school equiv.
13 Famous frontiersman
14 Luxury car
15 Certain Semite
17 Actor Kathy or Alan
18 P __ "pneumatic"
19 Garrison of tennis
20 CPR giver
21 Adverse reactions
24 Earth tone
26 Shop tools
27 Argentine plain
29 Amidst
31 Rope fiber
32 Stylish
33 Goes down
37 Actor Erwin
38 Devotion
41 *You __ There*
42 Cook's portions: Abbr.
44 Talk wildly
45 Footnote abbr.
47 Slammer
49 Three-wheelers
50 F to F, e.g.
53 Encrusted
54 Back-row cry
57 CD-__ (computer device)
60 Oklahoma city
61 Comet part
62 Muscat resident
64 Slender bristle
65 Russian designer
66 Communion piece
67 Fashion monogram
68 Performs
69 Crook's "soup"

DOWN

1 Singer Lane
2 Sand, silt and clay
3 "Cheers!"
4 French article
5 Military eatery
6 Razor filler
7 __ to the occasion
8 Girlfriend: Fr.
9 Be at loggerheads
10 Newspaper name
11 Author Segal
12 *Inferno* poet
16 Mingus' instrument
22 Tax agcy.
23 Modern communications machine
25 Numbers cruncher: Abbr.
27 "Hey, you!"
28 River islands
29 __-you note
30 Shrivel
32 Greenish blue
34 1991 Ron Howard film
35 Creamy cheese
36 Puts in place
39 Got one's bearings
40 Site of Cornwallis' surrender
43 Big stink
46 Boston cream __
48 56, in old Rome
49 Catch some rays
50 Poet's tributes
51 __ Island, NY
52 Gibes
53 Nat and Natalie
55 Betting game
56 Religious ceremony
58 Unique fellow
59 Spanish painter
63 A month in Montmartre

BEASTLY

by Eileen Lexau

ACROSS

1 Showed up
5 Ravine
10 '60s hair style
14 Tel __
15 Separated
16 City map
17 Supreme Court number
18 Naive ones
19 Left, on a ship
20 Snoozed a bit
22 Mystery board game
23 "This is only __"
24 Off one's nut
26 Gridders' org.
28 Composer Rorem
29 Bandleader Brown
32 Rock-band tour assistant
34 Soup cracker
37 Track event
38 Doesn't have much food
41 __ mater
42 Put up
43 Peggy Fleming, e.g.
45 Berry or Kercheval
46 Prevent
49 Kazakhstan, once: Abbr.
50 Soap ingredients
53 Not a soul
55 Convent room
57 Fortunate ones
60 Palo __, CA
61 Was wearing
62 Look leeringly at
63 Courage
64 In a __ (excited)

65 Civil disturbance
66 Symphony woodwind
67 High-strung
68 Mtg.

DOWN

1 High-kicking dance
2 Navigate the air
3 Manufactured coins
4 Ties the score
5 Irving character
6 "__ and Away" (5th Dimension song)
7 Tag
8 Statement of belief
9 Elevs.
10 Not theoretical: Abbr.
11 Flatfish
12 Exalted
13 Baseball great Mel
21 Map book
22 Bill's partner
25 Produce
27 Allow
30 Mystery writer Queen
31 Cooking direction
33 Amongst
34 RBI, e.g.
35 "I Like __"
36 Place for a tie
38 Fraternal group
39 Almond-flavored liqueur
40 Rochester's boss
41 Burro
44 Building extension
46 __-woogie
47 North Americans, to Latinos
48 Bowling-alley buttons
51 Fill with happiness
52 North African nation
54 Smells
56 Come in second
58 Barracks beds
59 Leg joint
60 "Long __ and Far Away"
61 FDR's third veep

85 WATERLOGGED

by Shirley Soloway

ACROSS

1 The Charles' pet
5 Words before "happens" or "were"
9 "__ the night before . . ."
13 Turns to the right
14 Warwick and Westheimer
16 In this spot
17 Experiencing bad trouble
19 "I cannot tell __"
20 Wise goddess
21 Lubricated again
23 Enter, as a crowd
26 Crafty
27 Unworkable item
30 Part in a play
31 Tide type
33 Run off to wed
35 Memorable times
37 MacMurray or Allen
40 "__ Laurie" (Scottish air)
41 CPA's forte
42 Every 24 hours
43 Echelon
44 Throw out a line
45 Corbin on *L.A. Law*
46 1994, e.g.
48 Sty cry
50 Automotive fuel
51 Recede
53 Hustler's hangout
56 Disney production
58 Doing nothing
62 Clarinet cousin
63 Holds off
66 Writer Uris
67 As of
68 Point out
69 Wapitis
70 Retains after expenses
71 Pay attention to

DOWN

1 Water in Juárez
2 Labor Day mo.
3 Hebrew letter
4 Fire remains
5 Jockey Eddie
6 Big __, CA
7 Resident suffix
8 Unit of heat
9 East Asian
10 Fountainhead
11 Sharon of Israel
12 Run-down
15 Bolts of wool
18 Menu item
22 Single
24 Actress Verdugo
25 Pressurized container
27 Costly
28 Arm bone
29 Free-for-all
32 At a distance
34 Food fish
36 Up and about
38 Kazan of Hollywood
39 Changes color
42 Half of ND
44 Thieves
47 Mil. address
49 Looped ropes
51 School: Fr.
52 Biblical city
54 __ a million
55 Bandleader Miller
57 Change for a twenty
59 Theater award
60 Fill up
61 Spotted
64 Compass pt.
65 Interest amt.

by Fred Piscop

ACROSS

1 Sharp ache
5 Circuit
10 __ Eban
14 Like two peas in __
15 Island nation
16 Do another hitch
17 *Mikrokosmos* composer
19 Fourth planet
20 Unvoiced
21 Beginning stage
23 __ Na Na
24 Genesis album of 1981
26 Pole-vaulter Sergei
29 Road sign
30 *The Woman __* (Wilder film)
33 "__ live and breathe!"
34 Sweet wine
37 Power, in combinations
38 __-de-sac
39 "Open sesame" speaker
41 Tempe sch.
42 Newsman Marvin
44 Egyptian talisman
45 Well-used pencil
46 As __ a fox
48 CPR expert
49 Fills to the gills
51 Fictional Starr
53 Go for apples, perhaps
54 '50s pitcher Ralph

56 Popular dolls
60 Knowledge
61 Baseball star
64 LL.B. holder
65 '60s tune, e.g.
66 Godunov was one
67 Lads
68 More meanspirited
69 Some turkeys

DOWN

1 Sunscreen ingredient
2 *Planet of the __*
3 __ contendere
4 Solidarity city
5 Appliance name
6 Trade center
7 Diner offering
8 Skater Midori
9 __ powder (run off)
10 Uniform accessory
11 Long-time coach at 24 Down
12 __ the hatchet
13 Lhasa __
18 Grand __ Island (vacation spot)
22 Sprint rival
24 Dixie state
25 He married Bacall
26 Supports
27 "The __" (regular's bar order)
28 Player of small parts?
29 Prepared apples, perhaps

31 Follow
32 Smears paint
35 Pacino et al.
36 Lawyers' org.
40 Suck up
43 Rubble and Fife
47 Dry, as wine
50 Comic Bud
52 Natterer, to Agnew
53 Anacin rival
54 Spill the beans
55 __-Rooter
56 Soft cheese
57 __ many words
58 Dutch cheese
59 Baltic states, once: Abbr.
62 In the manner of
63 Ave. crossers

87 DELIVERANCE

by Ann Seidel

ACROSS

1 Cellist __ Ma
5 "__ Nice Clambake" (*Carousel* tune)
10 Use the molars
14 Repute
15 Bagel relative
16 Sign of sanctity
17 Overwhelming victory
18 Wears
19 Moslem honorific
20 Ens' preceders
21 Old mail system
23 Tennis star Chris
25 Young bird of prey
26 Talk-show groups
28 Singer Taylor __
30 Gide or Previn
31 Painter Claude
32 Shade source
35 Meek one
36 Hankered
37 French girlfriend
38 Sault __ Marie, Ontario
39 Big, noisy bird
40 Spring up
41 Chores
42 Carve in stone
43 Costello's foil
46 Windowpane adhesive
47 Gridiron tactic
50 Non-commercial notice: Abbr.
53 Birch or beech
54 Buenos __, Argentina
55 Weaving machine
56 Angler's aid
57 Bullwinkle, for one
58 __ of Wight
59 Tabulates
60 Back-of-the-book reference
61 English prep school

DOWN

1 The old days
2 Baseball's Blue Moon
3 Sam Cooke song
4 Food scrap
5 Loathes
6 Cheerful
7 Like pie, perhaps?
8 Skin moisturizer
9 Sharp-sighted
10 Use Visa
11 Actress Veronica
12 "Für __"
13 Least desirable
21 Soccer great
22 Breathe hard
24 Action word
26 Bosom friends
27 Med. school subject
28 Portuguese titles
29 From the top
31 Singer Jagger
32 Miss Manners predecessor
33 Talk like Daffy Duck
34 __ the Press
36 Deli beef
37 In __ (stuck)
39 __ Hari
40 Stops procrastinating
41 Shower linen
42 English region
43 Entertainers' union
44 Yawning
45 Animal category
46 Bel __ cheese
48 "Runaround Sue" singer
49 Urge on
51 Napoleon or Han
52 Prayer finish
55 Untruth

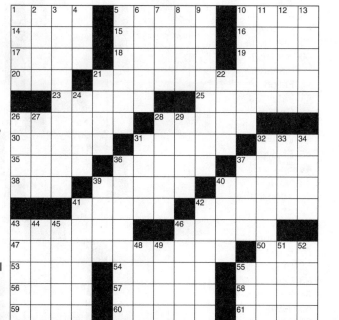

88 FOUR-BAGGER

by Ann Seidel

ACROSS

1 Rhyme scheme
5 Lively
9 Actress Jaclyn
14 Late singer/ politico Sonny
15 Hint
16 Sierra Nevada lake
17 "Do __ others . . ."
18 Actress Lenska
19 Lasso
20 Traveler's bags
22 Born first
23 Forgo
24 Booby __
26 *Joie de vivre*
29 __ out (exposes)
33 Hunger hankerings
37 Nuclear-warhead acronym
39 Arm bone
40 Baseball manager Felipe
41 Irate
42 Corp. bigshots
43 Aquatic bird
44 Wallet fillers
45 Enjoys gum
46 Sparse
48 Not faked
50 Abominable Snowman
52 Bahamas seaport
57 Bring about
60 Student bags
63 Open a bottle
64 Window ledge
65 Yawn inducer
66 *La __ Vita*
67 Actress Adams
68 __ about (approximately)
69 Plumber's tool
70 Catches forty winks
71 Sawbucks

DOWN

1 Treat badly
2 Employee's reward
3 Prank
4 Phone enclosure
5 Sloppy John Hancock
6 Definite asset
7 Hold sway
8 Bread necessity
9 Small river
10 Postal bag
11 "If __ a Hammer"
12 Carry around
13 Listen to
21 Mediocre grades
25 Invitation letters
27 Prayer conclusion
28 Saltpeter part
30 Swiss modernist
31 "Ah, Wilderness were Paradise __!"
32 Give lip to
33 Butter squares
34 Actor Baldwin
35 Nick Charles' mate
36 Burlap bag
38 Artful dodge
41 Pitcher __ Wilhelm
45 Show approval
47 Indian dwelling
49 Places for some bracelets
51 Norwegian dramatist
53 Wooden shoe
54 British biscuit
55 Buckeye State city
56 Manipulative people
57 Cows masticate them
58 Soon
59 Home of the Bruins
61 Verdi opera
62 Paper fastener

89 WONDERFUL

by Norma Steinberg

ACROSS

1 Coke and Pepsi, e.g.
6 "Yay, maestro!"
11 Actor Mineo
14 Scene of the action
15 Caesar or Brutus
16 Opposite of sing.
17 Majestic ending
19 Shade tree
20 Run in neutral
21 Convene
22 *NYPD Blue* character
23 Actress Lansbury
26 Dress fabric
28 Pavement material
29 Implant
33 Farrow or Sara
34 "Little piggie"
35 South Sea island
36 D-sharp alias
39 "__ corny as Kansas . . ."
41 Inventor Howe
43 Put away alphabetically
44 Referred to
46 Burt's ex
47 Sermon subject
48 Patriotic org.
49 Nos. for athletes
51 Holyfield feat: Abbr.
52 Happy faces
55 Posse member, e.g.
57 "*Mazel __!*"
58 Sea plea
60 Impoverished
61 Yalie
62 Food source
67 Total (up)
68 Employment
69 "High Noon" singer
70 Caustic liquid
71 Sharp pains
72 *Riders to the Sea* playwright

DOWN

1 Droop
2 Hockey great
3 Antidrug org.
4 __ *Get Your Gun*
5 Equestrian gear
6 Cheese-store choice
7 Howard or Reagan
8 *Amo, __, amat*
9 Legally binding
10 Former
11 Neurologists and OB-GYNs
12 Apportion
13 Like bad gravy
18 Afire, in a restaurant
23 Storage room
24 Wynonna's mother
25 Rocky Mountain watershed
27 Get one's goat
30 Spheres
31 Prufrock's creator
32 Dors or Sands
37 Share and share __
38 Choir voice
40 Close an envelope
42 *Roseanne* or *Coach*
45 Put on the Ritz
50 Sand bars
52 Unbelievable bargain
53 Like old bread, perhaps
54 The March King
56 Display
59 Straddle
60 Corporate exec.
63 Omelet ingredient
64 Family reunion attendees
65 School subj.
66 Casual shirt

90 GHOULISH TIMES

by Dean Niles

ACROSS

1 Cry like a baby
5 Mrs. Gorbachev
10 Pops
14 Sore spot
15 Boo-boo
16 Drama award
17 Rock group
19 Step to the __
20 El Salvador neighbor
21 *The Most Happy* __
22 Stimpy's pal
23 __ in (get closer)
25 *Hair* star
31 Defeated overwhelmingly
33 Did a garden chore
34 Lah-di-__
35 Poker contribution
36 Coal enclosure
37 *The Thin Man* woman
38 Favorite
39 Window ledge
41 James Bond's nemesis
43 Deceptive remark
46 Get up
47 Hippie home
48 Jazz form
51 Work periods
56 Gabor and Perón
57 Date arrangement
59 Belgrade resident
60 Car pedal
61 Where the gold is

62 Do in
63 Bottomless pit
64 Astronaut Shepard

DOWN

1 Speed-of-sound name
2 Sound reflection
3 "Where or __"
4 Starring role
5 Certain tire
6 Downright
7 Rainbow
8 Part of ASPCA
9 Early vessel
10 Money
11 Cain's brother
12 "Don't touch that __!"
13 Antitoxins
18 Blender result
21 Crease
23 __ National Park, Utah
24 Spanish cheer
25 __-frutti
26 Blvd., e.g.
27 In a __ (later)
28 Embellish
29 The red planet
30 Former Irani leader
31 Transported
32 Unique fellow
36 Down in the dumps
37 Modernist
39 Jump over
40 Mensa measures
41 Hides away

42 The thick of things
44 Bing or David
45 Little bits
48 Armstrong or Myerson
49 Daredevil Knievel
50 Actress Theda
51 Stick around
52 __ la Douce
53 Trompe l'__ (visual deception)
54 Granny
55 Submachine gun
57 Trade-name abbr.
58 City, informally

91 WEAR AM I?

by Norma Steinberg

ACROSS

1 Collins or Donahue
5 "My Way" singer
9 Endow with godhood
14 Author Jaffe
15 Appear to be
16 Additional
17 "__ Around" (Beach Boys song)
18 Montreal baseballer
19 Buffalo kin
20 North Carolina area
23 Way in
24 Conflicts
28 Literary selection
32 __ de France
33 Started the PC
37 Leather with a nap
39 "Natural" hairdo
40 Shatter
43 Plant stand?
44 Falls in drops
46 Reason for overtime
48 Sense of self
49 Symphony conductor
52 Thickly
54 In __ (neither here nor there)
59 Prodigies' opposites
63 George Burns prop
66 Weaving machine
67 __-a-brac
68 Up
69 Early Peruvian
70 M*A*S*H star
71 Gas-powered bike
72 Way out
73 Bambi, e.g.

DOWN

1 Cost
2 __'s Heroes
3 Bumbling
4 "See ya!"
5 On a cruise
6 Barber's cry
7 Retained
8 One-celled animal
9 Campaign events
10 Be
11 __ Always Fair Weather ('55 film)
12 To and __
13 PBS' __ Can Cook
21 Exaggeration
22 Scott Joplin creation
25 Try to deceive
26 __ statesman
27 "Come up and __ sometime"
29 Help-wanted notices
30 Total
31 Shoe coverings
33 Revealed
34 Coming __ in Samoa
35 Celestial hunter
36 Heavy weight
38 Western sch.
41 Pose
42 That girl
45 Bedaubed
47 Perform alone
50 High, in music
51 Place for shadow
53 Quench
55 Phrase from a Michael Jackson tune
56 Singer Haggard
57 Newlywed
58 Felix's roommate
60 Cher's surname, once
61 In __ parentis
62 General Bradley
63 Projection on a wheel
64 __ Jima
65 Wide divergence

ACROSS

1 Saudi citizen
5 Tortoiselike
9 Own up
14 Libertine
15 Mandlikova of tennis
16 Weepy
17 "Bye-bye!"
18 In a while
19 Weasel relative
20 Misleading device
23 Navy VIP
24 Art Deco name
25 Hurries off
27 South American rodent
30 Tumult
32 Woke up
33 Food store, for short
34 Western alliance
37 British title
38 Hot under the collar
41 Berry or Kercheval
42 Author of *The Nazarene*
44 Crimson and cerise
45 Perfect
47 Employers
49 With an even hand
50 Composer Mahler
52 __ *Misbehavin'*
53 Soldiers' org.
54 July 4 noisemaker
60 City dept.
62 Astringent
63 Mata __
64 Parisian wild cat
65 Distribute, with "out"
66 Ardor
67 1987 world champion figure skater
68 Jury member
69 Writing place

DOWN

1 Cultural pursuits
2 Wander about
3 Roadster
4 Lab vessels
5 California peak
6 Galahad's weapon
7 __ about (approximately)
8 Diminish
9 Like some modern music
10 P.I.
11 Dolly Levi, e.g.
12 Dunne or Papas
13 Novices
21 Eastern Indians
22 Comedian Murphy
26 __ Jose, CA
27 Space agcy.
28 Writer Leon
29 Heartsick ballads
30 Necklace units
31 Shade trees
33 Forest forager
35 Blue-green
36 "My One and __"
39 Fountain of Rome
40 Singer Ross
43 Big success
46 Jilted
48 Ceiling support beam
49 More solid
50 Zest
51 United competitor, formerly
52 Keen
55 Incline
56 Gen. Robert __
57 Leafy green
58 Distinctive periods
59 Ice arena
61 Dudgeon

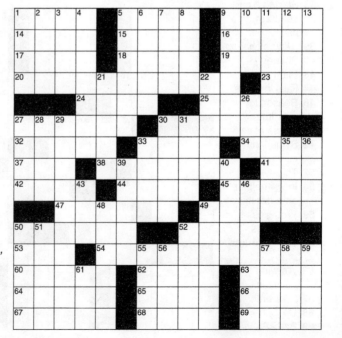

93 BOARING

by Dean Niles

ACROSS

1 Shop shaper
6 Roseanne's surname, once
10 Music-score notation
14 Collection
15 Sheriff Andy's son
16 Tortoise competitor
17 Lowlife
18 Alight
19 __-de-camp
20 Part of M.I.T.
21 Senate bill of a sort
23 Skulks
25 Pick, with "for"
26 Good __ Policy
30 "__ was saying . . ."
33 Forest clearing
36 Chess piece
37 Nerve
38 Split apart
39 Fish-eating eagle
40 Fable ender
41 In the course of
42 Floral vessel
43 Chicago airport
44 "Certainly!"
45 Decisive defeat
47 Funding source in D.C.
48 Christmas quaff
52 Uninformed buy
58 Had on
59 Pure black
60 __ bene
61 Blend
62 To be, to Babette
63 Potter's need
64 Escapee
65 __ and die
66 Cellist Ma
67 Mix up

DOWN

1 Endures
2 Senator Specter
3 In a __ (quickly)
4 Clumsy
5 Take a gander at
6 Western tie
7 On __ with (equal to)
8 Skating floor
9 Women's magazine
10 Map
11 Hideaway
12 "Das Lied von der __" (Mahler work)
13 Experience
21 Tire-pressure inits.
22 Tax mo.
24 Supercool
27 *The __ Gatsby*
28 Flicka, for one
29 Goof
30 Heavenly glow
31 Headliner
32 Man or Capri
33 Overcast
34 Whitewash component
35 Hertz competitor
37 Run riot
40 Synthesizer eponym
42 Motel sign
45 Pallid
46 Spike or Bruce
47 TV-screen element
49 Famous
50 Bay window
51 Comedy or tragedy, e.g.
52 Yeats or Keats
53 Absorbed by
54 Stabilizer, for short
55 Mallet sport
56 Buckwheat's affirmative
57 Flatten in the ring
61 Rural grp.

ACROSS
1 Shoots out
6 Worry
10 First-grade lesson
14 Yankee Yogi
15 Take out, to an ed.
16 Perry's creator
17 Loss of creative talent
19 100 dinars
20 Return addressee
21 West or Clarke
22 Folklore meanie
23 Love god
25 Hoards
27 Break of day
30 Corrida shout
32 Pigeonhole
33 Touched down
34 Egyptian cotton
36 Martini additive
39 __ Vegas
40 Cosmetic-pencil target
42 Female deer
43 Lying still
45 Tim of *WKRP*
46 Spill the beans
47 Coin . . .
49 . . . and its color
50 Ingests
51 Positive
54 Ward of *Sisters*
56 Actor Sharif
57 Puppy bite
59 Ferguson and Miles
63 *Of __ and Men*
64 Wise investors
66 Chase of films
67 River in Spain

68 Corn concoctions
69 "__ la vie!"
70 Told a tall tale
71 Little fish

DOWN
1 Recedes
2 Like a pittance
3 Where to spend 19 Across
4 Neptune's staff
5 More logical
6 Four-term pres.
7 Paper pack
8 Inventor Howe
9 Principles
10 Pressurized can

11 Inspired thought
12 County in Ireland
13 Monica of tennis
18 Sagging
24 More wily
26 In the ship's hold
27 Spanish surrealist
28 Greenspan or Shepard
29 Sarcastic remarks
31 Burning particle
35 First zodiac sign
37 Electrical unit
38 Morays
40 Sicilian hot spot

41 Most unusual
44 Fall back
46 Specialized restaurant
48 Christmas tree enhancement
51 Humorous
52 Author Zola
53 Rain clouds
55 Nightstand items
58 Remove a covering
60 Jackson or Meara
61 Command to Rover
62 Meth.
65 Serling of suspense

95

APT NAMES

by Norma Steinberg

ACROSS

1 Church service
5 Hayworth or Coolidge
9 Economic indicator: Abbr.
12 "So long, Pierre"
14 Japanese fare
15 __ *Bravo* (John Wayne film)
16 He's a Hollywood bigwig
18 Years: Fr.
19 Maine town
20 Sing like Ella
21 Forum garments
24 Nicks or Wonder
26 *Greed* and *Intolerance*, e.g.
28 Yangtze boat
31 Desertlike
32 Diner sign
35 Chelsea, to Roger
36 Washroom: Abbr.
37 Hawaii components
39 Fish eggs
40 Skilled
42 Buffalo's water
43 Condor or finch
44 Flotsam and jetsam
46 Clientele
48 Allergic reactions
51 Byways
52 Stick around
54 Kicks out
56 Follower of Attila
57 She's got great hands
62 Where to see *Spin City*
63 Clarinetist Shaw
64 Poet Dickinson
65 "Gotcha!"
66 Strong __ ox
67 Mayberry moppet

DOWN

1 Leader met by Nixon
2 Public notices
3 [Not my mistake]
4 Bering __
5 Ladder steps
6 *Once __ Enough* (Susann novel)
7 "__ a Small Hotel"
8 Tire filler
9 She'll be patient
10 Columbus' smallest ship
11 Hitching __
13 Of the city
14 Sermon subject
17 Spends foolishly
20 __ Valley, CA
21 Temper tantrum
22 She's a peacemaker
23 H.S. diploma alternative
25 Moving vehicles
26 Pre-entrée course
27 Vendition
29 Squirrel food
30 Requisites
33 Roofing material
34 Trim the bangs, e.g.
37 "How sweet __!"
38 Absence
41 Speak to God
43 Swimsuit part
45 Clippers
47 ". . . __ the Wizard"
49 Webber/Rice opus
50 Stay-put protest
52 Pahlavi's title
53 Oompah horn
55 Fidel's co-revolutionary
57 Fed. airport monitor
58 __, *amas, amat*
59 Pitcher part
60 Actor Wallach
61 Bar or bakery order

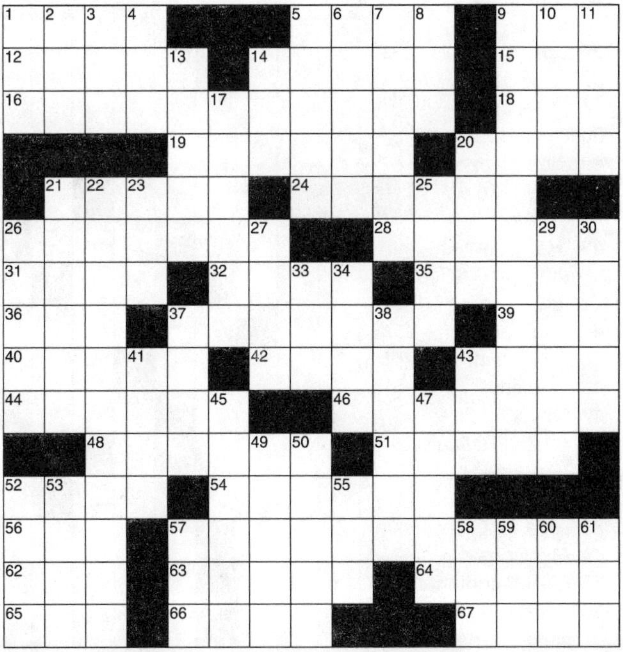

by Lee Weaver

ACROSS

1 They play for pay
5 Large aquatic mammal
10 Singe
14 *Charley's __*
15 Music hall
16 Angel topper
17 Breakfast fare
19 Muslim religious leader
20 Stadia
21 Cravat holder
23 Conks out
25 Beer mug
26 Appalling
29 Hibachi residue
31 Fix the sound track again
34 Instrument for a Marx brother
35 Grande or Bravo
36 Spanish coin
37 *__ Ventura: Pet Detective*
38 Diminishes
40 Sloe __ fizz
41 Acted like a dictator
43 "Here Comes the __" (Beatles tune)
44 Stare at
45 Pelvic joint
46 __ diem
47 Melts together
48 A Little Rascal
51 Very dry, as champagne
53 Area for Old MacDonald
55 Quiver contents
59 With 64 Across, John Wayne film
60 Breakfast fare
62 Sponsorship
63 Official proclamation
64 See 59 Across
65 Learning method
66 Errata
67 "I'm all __"

DOWN

1 Sobriquet for Hemingway
2 Regretful one
3 In the past
4 __ and be counted
5 Mountie's mount
6 Altar response
7 Pepper with pebbles
8 Spit and __
9 Beginning
10 Hot peppers
11 Breakfast fare
12 "Too bad!"
13 Frolic boisterously
18 Carpenter's need
22 Goddess of grain
24 Spoke
26 Moby Dick seeker
27 Texas city
28 Breakfast fare
30 Toper
32 Practical
33 Bêtes noires
35 Eric the __
36 Bill-signing need
38 Answer an invitation
39 Sidewalk's edge
42 Like Anna's King
44 Abominable act
46 Send-up
47 Roll up, as a flag
48 Later than
49 Slow and majestic, in music
50 Aspect
52 River floaters
54 Faucet problem
56 Gumbo ingredient
57 River dam
58 De Gaulle arrivals
61 Sgt., e.g.

OVER YOUR HEAD

by Fred Piscop

ACROSS

1 Violet variety
6 Indy 500 entrant
11 Hole-punching gadget
14 Teddy Roosevelt's daughter
15 Athens marketplace
16 Cedar Rapids college
17 Mars phenomenon
19 __ Sharkey (Rickles sitcom)
20 Appear
21 Skating place
22 It's a wrap
24 Sole-related
27 Deserve
28 Dash competitor
31 Take advantage of
32 Track figure
34 Sam of *Jurassic Park*
36 More despicable, perhaps
39 Racetrack event
43 Dreamy state
44 Hall of Famer Banks
45 Modify text
46 Opening Day mo.
48 CIA precursor
49 DeVito series
52 Most lemonlike
55 1936 Olympics star
57 Actress Swenson
58 Dynamic start
62 Poor review
63 Leo G. Carroll role
66 In favor of
67 Starts the pot
68 Source of annoyance
69 Sun Yat-__
70 Irascible
71 Lock of hair

DOWN

1 Soft foods
2 __ vera
3 Aswan Dam site
4 Rascal
5 Law or saw ender
6 Wisconsin city
7 Ten-percenter
8 Crested parrot
9 Bullpen ace's stat
10 Hard knocks
11 Ghana's capital
12 Tom of *The Dukes of Hazzard*
13 Sierra __
18 Tax-deferred accts.
23 More pretentious
25 Put to sleep
26 Red horse
28 "__ how!"
29 Impolite look
30 Lawn chemical
33 Milkers' handfuls
35 "__ Bloom"
36 Popular June gift
37 Mr. Rubik
38 Slugger's stats
40 Eye part
41 Followers of Josip Broz
42 "Permission granted!"
46 Merchant ship
47 Bog material
49 Baseball card company
50 Cognizant
51 Noble gas
53 Not dealt with
54 Slender candle
56 Command to Socks
59 Fencer's weapon
60 Guns the engine
61 Galena et al.
64 Singleton
65 Make a choice

by Shirley Soloway

ACROSS

1 Trunk item
6 Took off
10 Dick and Jane's dog
14 Attacks
15 Rajah's wife
16 Forum wear
17 Coarse-leafed vegetables
19 Manages, with "out"
20 Monty Hall offering
21 Individual
22 Goes along
24 __-of-mouth
26 Sidelong glances
27 African desert
30 Baseball's __ Fame
32 Tactics
33 Circle of light
34 Vocalized
37 Response from space
38 Japanese island
41 Mil. officer
42 Footfall
44 Prepares the press
45 Actress Garbo
47 Leaveners
49 Did farm work
50 Mimics
51 Shopping aid
52 The Bunkers' daughter
53 Ventilate
54 Levin and Gershwin
58 Gardening tool
59 Swimming motion
62 Singer Ed
63 Money in Milan
64 Varnish ingredient
65 Young men
66 Heavenly spot
67 Birth cert., e.g.

DOWN

1 Roe source
2 Trim, as expenses
3 The Charles' terrier
4 Train line
5 List-ending abbr.
6 Palm branch
7 Ontario or Michigan
8 Map dir.
9 Refuse, as testimony
10 Sound systems
11 Expressionless
12 S-shaped moldings
13 Soviet news agency
18 Circle dance
23 Solidify
25 Approximately
27 Dieters' retreats
28 Greatly
29 Alley Cat step
30 *Philadelphia* Oscar-winner
31 Word of woe
33 Suggestion
35 Short message
36 Happy
39 Ready for smooching
40 Matures
43 Noblewoman
46 No longer working
48 Hero of *Exodus*
49 Knightly addresses
50 Memorable mission
51 Compare
52 Snatch
53 Land measure
55 Billy or Pete
56 Related
57 Dispatched
60 Lend a hand
61 Prefix for angle or color

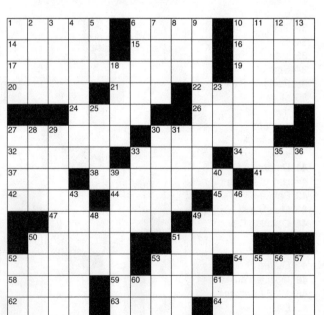

99 GO WITH THE FLOW

by Frank Gordon

ACROSS

1 Jazz singer Vaughan
6 Result of a conking
10 Angry
13 Inflationary __
15 Jacob's twin
16 Indefinite pronoun
17 Colonial silversmith
18 Puma's pad
19 Rap sheet abbr.
20 Dakar's country
22 Bee's quest
24 CD-__ (computer adjunct)
25 Inferior
27 Word with sell or shell
29 In a tizzy
30 Rub-__
34 Train unit
35 Naval rank: Abbr.
36 *Raising __* ('87 film)
38 "I'd like to propose __"
40 Lineup at Lillehammer
41 Horse-race measures
43 Bolger or Charles
44 Coll. basketball event
45 "¿*Cómo __ usted?*"
46 __ salts
48 Singer Lovett
49 Recite magic words
51 Wail
52 Horner's milieu
55 JFK or O'Hare
58 Gold, to Gomez
59 Stink
61 Ceylonese teas
63 *Krazy __*
64 Billy Budd's captain
65 Completely
66 Overhead trains
67 __ out (just got by)
68 Symbol

DOWN

1 Azerbaijan, once: Abbr.
2 Large primates
3 Reds' stadium, formerly
4 "We __ amused"
5 Seraglio
6 Starr et al.
7 Cable network
8 Having prevalent attitudes
9 Blender setting
10 Medieval defense
11 Pop singer Paul
12 Letter opener
14 Drumstick
21 Kal Kan rival
23 Fad
26 Vast expanse
27 Grocer's need
28 Author Joyce Carol __
29 In a tough spot
31 Free-for-all
32 Up to
33 Moisten meat
35 Winter time in Chi.
37 Garden climber
39 Once more
42 Bath or Bad Ems
43 French roast
47 Twisted and turned
48 Seek advice from
50 Brass
51 All in
52 Pepsi rival
53 Spoken
54 Decays
56 Troy, NY coll.
57 Head overseas?
60 Poetic preposition
62 "That's a joke, __"

100 COMMAND MEN

by Dean Niles

ACROSS

1 Ran in the wash
5 Ran easily
10 Take it easy
14 Helper
15 Sound off
16 A Great Lake
17 Use the scissors
18 Dreadlocked cultist
19 Swedish soprano
20 Ray Charles song
23 Corrida cry
24 Boston ballplayers, familiarly
25 Weasel relative
28 MTV viewer, typically
30 French friend
33 Woody Allen film
36 Register drawer
37 Give a squeeze
38 Creole vegetable
39 *Star Trek* order
44 Hardwood tree
45 Advocate
46 Black-and-white snacks
47 __-Cat (winter vehicle)
48 Canadian prov.
49 Disillusioned one's lament
57 Cotton holder
58 Unaffiliated company
59 Sunscreen chem.
60 Radar image
61 Punctuation mark
62 Component
63 "__ Sides Now"
64 In the matter of
65 Becomes firm

DOWN

1 Baroque composer
2 Leslie Caron film
3 Redact
4 Cabinet grp.
5 Rhine siren
6 "__ Ben Jonson"
7 El __, TX
8 Singer James
9 Scroll site
10 Chill out
11 Actor Roberts
12 Swim alternative
13 Newsman Koppel
21 Sacred
22 Folk singer Mitchell
25 Eavesdroppers
26 Islamic deity
27 Palliative
28 Stocking shade
29 Omelet ingredients
30 Seek permission
31 *The Bells of St. __*
32 "__ Believer" ('66 tune)
34 Gangster
35 Jot down
36 *TV Guide* abbr.
40 Paul of *Scarface*
41 Nin's works, e.g.
42 Subject matter
43 Table scraps
47 Slender one
48 Pungent plant
49 By oneself
50 Got off
51 Soon
52 Out of commission
53 Musical composition
54 Tarzan's partner
55 Newspaper notice
56 Grub
57 Consumer org.

ANSWERS

1

S	H	U	T		S	T	E	S		W	H	O	
T	A	P	E	S		L	I	T	E		C	H	O	W
A	S	H	E	N		U	N	D	E	R	L	I	N	E
	T	O	P	I	A	R	Y		S	E	A	L	E	D
		L	E	T	U	P		P	A	S	S	E	D	
I	N	S	E	C	T		L	E	W	I	S			
B	A	T		H	O	G	A	N		T	I	D	A	L
I	T	E	M		S	E	C	T	S		C	O	C	A
D	O	R	I	C		N	E	A	P	S		W	R	Y
	S	L	I	E	R		A	T	O	N	E	S		
	L	A	T	I	N	S		S	T	A	N	G		
C	O	G	E	N	T		T	A	S	T	E	R	S	
O	V	E	R	G	R	O	W	N		O	M	A	H	A
P	E	N	S		O	V	I	D		R	A	D	O	N
E	R	A			S	A	G	S			N	E	W	T

2

HAZY · CHILI · SCAM
OBIE · HAVOC · HALO
CLOSEONESEYESTO
KEN · LOOS · WALKON
DESI · CALL
INLOVE · GATE · FCC
MAINE · PURE · AREA
PINONESEARSBACK
EVER · VAST · LOUIE
LEN · HILT · CUDDLY
HELM · PAGE
ACCORD · PANG · PJS
THUMBONESNOSEAT
TOBE · ERASE · POPE
AWAY · RAKES · ANEW

3

CARP · ABASH · CHAR
ALOU · BOCCI · RENO
PAULNEWMAN · ENTO
PRESET · ENDEARED
ASST · TUMMY
STETS · AMY · DOFFS
TALE · PLO · BEFORE
ALI · BALLOON · NEE
COWPER · LLB · SDAK
KNARS · RYE · TEAKS
LOOSE · ODOR
ALLSTATE · EDMUND
REAP · GARYCOOPER
ANCE · APLEA · NORA
BOHR · SEEPY · SNOW

4

BLAH · MIRED · ABBA
OOZE · ERASE · TIER
SOURGRAPES · ITEM
CPR · LENT · PALTRY
HYENAS · BITTE
ARTHOUSE · REV
HASTE · INGE · MELS
ERAT · SCALD · ANSI
ALLY · OKIE · INDEX
TOT · ABERRANT
WILEY · VEALER
SPARER · STAR · ONE
LUTE · SWEETTOOTH
OMEN · UINTA · ASEA
PARE · PATER · SERB

5

AGES · RAVES · ATTA
MOLE · ALIKE · SWAB
PAIROFACES · TIRE
STAIR · NEST · ANTS
AMISS · EMIT
LADLES · STAROF
EROS · ABUT · MEWLS
STU · TWOTONE · EEE
TIBER · NAPE · TRAM
ELAINE · AGASSI
ERGO · HELEN
ATTN · OLEG · NAILS
SOIE · SINGINGDUO
POMS · ELIOT · ELMS
STET · STENO · REPO

6

CORN · BASIC · EPEE
ABOO · AROMA · SODA
MOUSETRAPS · STIR
PEEWEE · RETREATS
ELSA · LEANT
TOGAS · PAS · SCORN
HURT · HES · SPECIE
ATE · EARTHLY · HOW
IDEALS · ROY · PITS
SONGS · BOB · TIPSY
AGILE · OFIT
INCREASE · RECAPS
TIRE · BUNKERHILL
ONES · ORDIE · ERIE
NESS · RESTS · DYED

7

ALAS · OHARA · CHUB
SADE · RATON · HARI
SIMMERDOWN · OLGA
ANAIL · AMS · FIFES
DENTISTS · CURB
EAT · FORBADE
LEE · SEALED · OKRA
ELMS · AMEND · YEAR
ABBE · MIDDLE · DBL
PARADED · EDS
OWED · BADGERED
TRIAL · FAR · ENOLA
MALL · BOILEDOVER
EVEL · RAZES · RECT
NEDS · AMENS · ARTS

8

ABCS · CIRCA · ORAL
DOLE · ODIUM · RARE
ONEARMEDBANDITS
BSA · AMASS · TAN
EARSHOT · CHICLE
SISI · NEATH · NOOK
LIS · LION · ACE
TWOCENTSWORTH
IRE · INRE · DNA
NESS · SARGE · TIER
KETTLE · ORLANDO
ERE · LIGHT · HID
THREELEGGEDRACE
IONA · ENOLA · ALTO
DESK · GORED · MESS

9

E	C	H	O		M	A	S	O	N		A	J	A	R
F	L	O	P		A	N	K	L	E		R	U	L	E
T	A	P	E		S	N	I	D	E		T	M	E	N
S	P	A	N		H	E	P		P	I	P	E	D	
		L	I	V	E		A	Z	A	L	E	A		
C	L	O	N	E	D		G	E	R	E		T	S	P
R	A	N	G	E		M	E	S	T	A		T	W	O
E	G	G	S		M	O	N	T	Y		S	H	E	S
S	E	C		C	O	N	E	Y		F	E	E	L	S
T	R	A		H	O	E	R		O	R	A	C	L	E
		S	I	E	S	T	A		B	A	C	H		
	V	I	S	O	R		T	A	J		H	A	I	G
E	D	I	T		L	O	I	R	E		E	N	R	Y
L	E	D	A		S	T	O	I	C		S	C	A	N
D	A	Y	S		D	O	N	A	T		T	E	N	T

10

R	I	G	E	L		P	E	E	R		A	B	C	S
A	D	O	R	E		E	L	E	E		P	I	L	E
G	E	O	R	G	E	S	A	N	D		O	L	I	N
S	A	P		A	T	O	M		B	A	L	L	O	T
			P	T	A	S		G	A	I	L	Y		
S	A	M	U	E	L		B	A	R	R	O	O	M	S
A	G	A	P	E		K	I	L	O	S		C	O	O
L	I	R	A		C	O	N	A	N		M	E	R	L
E	L	K		C	O	R	D	S		C	E	A	S	E
M	E	S	D	A	M	E	S		W	A	R	N	E	D
		T	A	M	P	A		C	A	N	E			
C	O	R	N	E	A		I	L	S	A		T	A	N
A	M	A	D		D	I	N	A	H	S	H	O	R	E
L	O	N	I		R	A	T	S		T	I	M	E	X
M	O	D	E		E	N	O	S		A	T	E	S	T

11

W	E	S	T		A	I	M	S			H	A	N	S
H	A	I	R		W	R	I	T		H	A	B	I	T
A	C	R	E		A	O	N	E		E	L	E	N	A
T	H	E	M	O	R	N	I	N	G	A	F	T	E	R
			O	S	E			R	P	M				
S	M	A	R	T		B	O	A		O	A	S	T	
I	O	N		I	M	P	E	N	D		O	F	N	O
D	O	G	D	A	Y	A	F	T	E	R	N	O	O	N
O	R	E	O		O	T	I	O	S	E		O	R	E
	N	E	L	L		P	E	T		V	O	T	E	R
				P	S	I			C	U	R			
N	I	G	H	T	A	N	D	T	H	E	C	I	T	Y
A	N	N	I	E		A	R	I	A		H	O	R	A
S	T	U	N	T		P	I	N	S		I	N	O	N
H	O	S	S		E	P	E	E		D	A	N	K	

12

B	E	L	L		D	E	B	S		E	B	S	E	N
O	L	E	O		A	E	R	O		L	O	T	T	O
B	E	A	C	H	H	E	A	D		L	O	R	A	N
S	E	R	I	A	L		A	L	I	B	I			
			R	I	A	S		A	S	O	N	G		
	A	N	I	M	A	T	E		D	O	O	G	I	E
I	G	O	R	S		E	A	T	E	N		B	A	N
A	L	O	E		S	A	T	E	S		F	E	N	D
N	E	D		R	E	M	I	T		D	R	A	T	S
S	A	L	T	E	D		N	O	T	I	O	N	S	
		M	E	U	S	E		G	N	A	T			
			S	L	U	R	P		U	T	M	O	S	T
S	H	O	A	L		A	S	T	R	O	D	O	M	E
C	O	U	N	T		C	H	O	U		C	L	O	D
H	O	P	E	S		E	Y	E	S		L	A	G	S

13

E	S	P	Y		A	G	A	L		A	G	R	A	
T	H	A	I		P	O	L	E	S		E	L	A	L
H	A	P	P	Y	E	V	E	N	T		G	A	I	L
E	R	A	S	E	R		S	T	O	L	I	D	L	Y
L	E	S		A	T	A		I	R	I	S	H		
			C	H	U	C	K	L	E	S		A	S	A
R	A	J	A		R	I	N			A	B	N	E	R
I	G	O	T		E	D	I	T	S		I	D	L	E
S	A	Y	S	O			F	E	E		B	S	A	S
E	R	R		G	L	E	E	C	L	U	B			
		I	D	E	A	S		S	T	R		R	O	C
A	N	D	R	E	T	T	I		Z	A	D	O	R	A
B	A	I	O		H	O	R	S	E	L	A	U	G	H
I	N	N	S		S	P	I	E	R		S	T	A	N
G	A	G	S			S	S	T	S		H	E	N	S

14

F	L	A	I	R		M	U	T	E		L	E	S	T
O	U	N	C	E		A	R	U	T		A	C	T	I
G	R	E	E	N	E	G	G	S	A	N	D	H	A	M
S	E	W		D	R	I	E	S		A	L	O	N	E
			N	E	G			L	A	T	E			
F	A	K	I	R		O	V	E	R	T		T	A	E
A	L	O	E		O	N	E		G	E	R	U	N	D
C	L	O	C	K	W	O	R	K	O	R	A	N	G	E
T	A	K	E	I	N		S	E	T		R	E	I	N
S	H	Y		M	E	L	O	N		M	E	D	E	S
			S	O	D	A			A	I	R			
A	S	I	A	N		S	H	A	R	K		T	A	P
Y	E	L	L	O	W	S	U	B	M	A	R	I	N	E
E	V	E	L		H	I	R	E		D	A	N	T	E
S	E	X	Y		Y	E	L	L		O	T	T	E	R

15

A	S	T	A		S	W	A	M	I		A	J	A	R
W	H	I	M		H	E	L	E	N		P	A	L	E
R	U	B	B	E	R	B	A	N	D		I	C	O	N
A	L	E		T	I	S	S	U	E		E	K	E	D
P	A	T	T	O	N		S	N	A	C	K			
			I	N	K	E	D		T	R	E	N	D	S
D	E	G	A	S		L	A	G	E	R		I	O	U
E	R	O	S		G	I	V	E	R		N	F	L	D
E	L	L		N	O	S	I	R		B	E	E	T	S
D	E	F	I	E	S		T	E	S	L	A			
			B	R	A	S	S		C	A	R	E	R	S
A	L	A	I		I	C	E	M	A	N		L	O	A
P	O	L	S		P	A	P	E	R	C	L	I	P	S
A	B	L	E		E	L	I	T	E		I	D	E	S
T	E	S	S		R	A	C	E	S		V	E	R	Y

16

S	L	O	P	E		H	O	B	O		M	O	L	T
A	I	D	A	N		E	V	E	L		O	L	E	O
T	R	E	N	T		R	E	A	D		O	M	A	N
E	A	R	T	H	W	O	R	M	S		N	O	V	A
			U	R	N			T	A	S	S	E	L	
B	R	A	S	S	Y		B	R	E	N	T			
L	O	T	T	E		S	O	U	R	C	R	E	A	M
T	O	M	A		G	L	O	B	S		U	L	N	A
S	T	E	R	I	L	I	Z	E		S	C	I	O	N
			S	L	I	M	E		T	O	K	E	N	S
	R	E	P	E	L	S		E	E	L				
E	L	L	A		S	U	N	G	L	A	S	S	E	S
P	A	A	R		A	S	E	A		C	U	T	I	E
O	T	I	C		D	E	A	D		E	V	E	N	T
S	E	T	H		E	R	R	S		D	A	W	E	S

17

R	E	E	S	E		A	M	E	S		M	O	R	T
C	A	R	T	A		N	A	V	E		A	R	E	A
A	R	G	O	T		T	R	E	E		T	R	E	X
P	O	P	E	Y	E	A	N	D	O	L	I	V	E	
			C	R	E	S	T		K	I	N	E	R	
A	C	C	O	S	T		A	M	A	N				
C	H	O	C		G	A	L	O	P		I	V	Y	
M	I	C	K	E	Y	A	N	D	M	I	N	N	I	E
E	P	A		M	E	S	T	A		U	C	L	A	
			S	A	S	H		E	S	T	H	E	R	
	A	M	A	T	I		S	A	N	E	R			
D	O	N	A	L	D	A	N	D	D	A	I	S	Y	
D	R	O	P		I	L	E	D		M	E	T	E	R
L	A	D	E		C	A	R	E		U	N	I	T	E
E	Y	E	S		K	I	D	D		S	T	R	I	P

18

S	P	A	S		S	I	R	S		R	O	P	E	D
P	A	S	T		T	R	I	P		O	P	E	R	A
A	S	H	E		R	O	N	A		M	A	T	E	S
W	H	E	E	L	A	N	D	D	E	A	L			
N	A	R	R	O	W		S	E	M	I		S	K	I
			U	S	A		I	N	S	P	A	N		
A	L	E	R	T		S	P	A	R	E	T	I	R	E
S	E	L	A		T	E	A	R	S		A	N	A	P
W	A	S	H	C	Y	C	L	E		B	R	E	N	T
A	R	I	S	E	S		A	M	A					
N	N	E		C	O	A	T		E	L	A	N	D	S
			R	I	N	G	S	I	D	E	S	E	A	T
S	P	O	I	L		R	A	G	U		S	E	R	A
T	A	R	S	I		E	R	O	S		E	D	I	T
A	T	S	E	A		E	S	T	A		T	Y	N	E

19

A	S	P	S		R	E	N	T		S	T	R	O	P
R	O	L	E		E	D	I	E		P	I	A	N	O
A	L	A	N		D	A	N	A		I	M	P	E	L
M	A	Y	D	A	Y	M	A	L	O	N	E			
I	C	E		V	E	E		N	E	S	T	L	E	
S	E	R	G	E		S	A	M	E		R	U	I	N
			E	R	G		R	O	I		O	B	O	E
S	O	S	Y	O	U	R	O	L	D	M	A	N		
S	A	B	U		S	P	A		L	O	A			
A	K	I	N		P	A	Y	S		U	N	C	L	E
N	E	E	D	L	E		E	G	G		A	A	R	
			H	E	L	P	M	E	R	H	O	N	D	A
C	O	H	E	N		L	O	G	O		P	A	D	S
A	W	A	I	T		A	N	E	W		E	P	E	E
P	E	S	T	O		T	O	R	N		N	E	R	D

20

H	I	C	C	U	P		V	E	T					
O	R	I	O	L	E		H	E	R	O		T	I	M
D	A	T	I	N	G		A	N	N	O		R	C	A
			I	F	A		G	R	E	E	N	M	A	I	L
A	D	Z	E		M	A	N	E	S		E	V	E	L
P	I	E	D	P	I	P	E	R		D	O	E	R	S
S	O	N		O	D	E	S		H	O	W	L		
E	N	S		P	A	R	S	L	E	Y		E	T	C
		A	S	P	S		R	A	R	E		R	H	O
P	A	R	T	Y		H	A	R	D	N	O	S	E	D
I	R	R	A		S	O	C	K	S		N	C	A	A
Q	U	E	B	E	C	O	I	S		A	S	H		
U	B	S		T	A	R	N		G	R	E	E	C	E
E	A	T		C	R	A	G		S	I	T	C	O	M
			H	E	Y		T	A	S	K	E	T		

21

G	O	T	O		I	Z	Z	Y			E	M	I	T
A	U	E	R		S	E	E	I	T		N	I	C	E
D	R	Y	C	L	E	A	N	E	R		I	N	O	N
			H	U	R	L		L	E	S	S	E	N	S
I	N	C	I	T	E		I	D	E	A	L	S		
T	A	R	D	E		I	N	S		L	E	W	D	
A	M	O	S		A	M	S		R	E	D	E	E	M
L	I	P		A	S	P	I	R	E	S		E	L	I
O	N	D	E	C	K		D	A	D		A	P	E	X
	G	U	R	U		J	E	T		S	I	E	T	E
	S	I	T	T	E	R		T	A	R	R	E	D	
S	E	T	T	E	E	S		A	I	L	S			
O	V	E	R		S	U	N	B	A	T	H	E	R	S
M	I	R	E		T	I	B	E	R		O	R	E	O
E	L	S	A		T	A	T	A		W	A	X	Y	

22

E	S	S	E		I	R	A			I	Q	S		
A	P	H	I	D		M	E	S	A		C	U	T	S
S	Q	U	E	E	Z	E	D	I	N		H	I	R	E
E	R	N	I	E	S		M	A	T	S		Z	E	E
			O	R	A	T	E		S	C	A	M	P	S
H	I	Q		E	Z	R	A		Y	O	G	A		
O	N	U	S		S	I	T	S		T	A	S	K	S
P	R	E	H	E	A	T		E	A	T	I	T	U	P
S	I	Z	E	S			E	S	P	N		N	E	R	O
	O	R	S	O		I	T	I	S		R	A	T	
T	I	N	M	E	N		G	A	M	E	R			
A	R	C		S	C	A	M		A	R	A	B	I	A
S	K	I	T		E	Q	U	A	L	I	Z	I	N	G
S	E	T	S		A	U	N	T		F	O	R	C	E
D	Y	E			A	D	E			R	D	A	S	

23

T	W	A		C	I	V	E	T		R	A	D	A	R
R	E	G		I	C	I	E	R		A	T	O	N	E
A	G	E		T	A	L	K	I	N	G	H	E	A	D
C	O	N	V	E	N	E		C	O	M	E	S	T	O
		E	T	T	A		S	T	Y	R	O	N		
	R	U	S	T	I	C			P	A	T	C	H	
A	T	T	I	R	E		P	L	O			E	A	U
S	I	N	G	I	N	G	T	E	L	E	G	R	A	M
I	C	U			D	O	O			D	R	A	I	N	S
A	S	T	A	R		V	E	S	S	E	L			
			P	A	L	E	S	T			O	S	A	Y
I	M	P	O	S	E	R		A	D	O	P	T	E	E
L	A	U	G	H	I	N	G	G	A	S		A	R	M
E	M	C	E	E		O	P	E	N	S		V	I	E
T	A	K	E	R		R	O	D	E	O		E	E	N

24

R	A	W		B	E	T	H		B	A	C	K	S	
E	L	A	M		E	P	E	E		A	T	R	I	A
A	O	N	E		V	I	A	L		T	E	E	N	Y
C	H	E	E	S	E	C	L	O	T	H		A	D	S
T	A	S	S	E	L			S	T	R	E	A	M	
			E	R	I	N			A	D	O	P	T	S
B	A	M		G	N	A	R	L			K	U	R	T
A	L	I		E	G	G	H	E	A	D		F	I	E
I	S	L	E		S	O	N	I	A		F	O	R	
T	O	K	E	N	S			A	R	L	O			
	G	R	A	T	I	S		C	A	R	O	L	S	
C	A	L		B	U	T	T	E	R	I	N	G	U	P
A	L	A	M	O		H	O	R	A		O	L	G	A
M	I	S	E	R		O	L	A	F		T	E	E	N
P	E	S	T	S		T	E	S	T		D	R	S	

25

W	I	L	D		A	R	O	M	A		T	S	A	R
A	S	E	A		G	E	L	I	D		A	P	S	O
N	E	A	R	A	T	H	A	N	D		D	E	C	O
T	E	P	I	D		E	V	E	L		A	O	K	
			N	A	P	A			R	E	T	O	R	T	S
A	R	C		M	I	T	L	A		I	S	H		
G	O	L	D	E	N		A	L	L	C	L	E	A	R
E	P	E	E		C	R	U	S	T		I	A	M	A
R	E	A	P	P	E	A	R		G	A	N	D	E	R
			R	O	O		G	A	L	E	N		S	S	A
A	B	A	T	I	N	G		E	N	D	S			
B	A	S		O	I	S	E		T	I	A	R	A	
A	R	M	S		T	E	A	R	S	O	F	J	O	Y
B	O	U	T		E	S	T	E	E		T	A	M	E
A	N	D	Y		S	T	E	R	N		S	R	A	S

26

P	A	P	A		A	P	S	O		A	T	I	M	E
A	V	E	R		L	A	I	R		S	I	R	E	S
L	I	K	E	G	A	N	G	B	U	S	T	E	R	S
E	V	E	A	R	D	E	N		S	E	A	N	C	E
			O	Y	L			G	U	R	N	E	Y	S
A	T	O	M	S			S	M	A	R	T			
M	O	R	A	S	S		E	S	P		I	P	S	O
P	U	L	L	O	U	T	T	H	E	S	T	O	P	S
S	T	Y	E		P	O	E			R	I	T	U	A	L
			S	P	A	R	K		T	O	R	S	O	
S	E	A	F	O	O	D		O	B	I				
I	N	L	E	T	S		E	B	O	N	I	Z	E	S
F	U	L	L	H	E	A	D	O	F	S	T	E	A	M
T	R	A	L	A		S	E	L	F		A	R	T	E
S	E	N	A	T		I	N	D	O		L	O	S	E

27

L	I	S	I		C	R	E	D	O		T	O	O	L
O	L	I	N		P	A	P	E	R		E	D	N	A
O	L	D	S		A	R	I	E	L		A	D	E	S
M	A	L	T	E	S	E	C	R	O	S	S			
S	T	E	E	L			S	N	A	P	A	T		
			P	L	I	E	D			N	O	V	A	E
D	O	T		A	N	G	O	R	A	G	O	A	T	S
U	V	E	A		G	A	Y	E	R		N	I	T	S
P	E	R	S	I	A	N	L	A	M	B		L	Y	E
E	R	R	E	D			E	D	S	E	L			
	T	E	N	O	R	S			S	A	D	I	E	
			S	I	A	M	E	S	E	T	W	I	N	S
E	D	I	E		D	A	V	I	D		S	E	T	S
L	E	N	O		I	L	E	N	E		O	G	R	E
L	E	A	F		O	L	S	E	N		N	O	O	N

28

A	M	O	S		G	A	R	D	E		A	M	E	N
D	O	N	T		A	L	I	E	N		G	A	M	E
A	R	I	A		B	E	G	E	T		E	X	I	T
M	A	C	R	O	S	C	O	P	I	C		I	T	S
S	N	E	E	R			R	E	R	U	N	S		
			C	A	P		R	E	B	U	K	E	S	
C	O	M	P	A	R	E	S			E	D	I	T	H
O	D	E	R		C	R	A	T	E		E	R	T	E
N	O	G	O	S		D	E	S	I	S	T	E	D	
G	R	A	N	T	E	E		D	E	L				
			B	E	E	T	L	E		S	A	M	M	S
S	M	U		M	U	L	T	I	R	A	C	I	A	L
T	A	C	O		D	E	N	N	Y		R	A	R	A
A	N	K	A		E	R	A	S	E		I	M	I	N
G	E	S	T		S	Y	S	T	S		D	I	E	T

29

A	L	A	N		J	A	Y			R	O	S	S	
O	L	I	V	E		O	N	O		L	E	A	H	S
N	A	M	E	O	F	A	D	D	R	E	S	S	E	E
E	R	E		N	A	N		A	U	D	I	T	S	
			D	A	K			N	O	D				
C	O	A	T	I	N	G		G	U	E	S	T	S	
N	U	M	B	E	R	A	N	D	S	T	R	E	E	T
A	R	I			N	A	E				I	R	E	
C	I	T	Y	S	T	A	T	E	A	N	D	Z	I	P
L	O	S	E	T	O		S	P	R	U	C	E	S	
			A	R	A			A	M	I				
T	O	R	E	S	T		I	C	E			J	A	M
U	S	P	O	S	T	A	L	S	E	R	V	I	C	E
M	A	I	L	S		L	I	L		A	M	B	E	R
P	R	E	D			L	E	E		L	I	E	D	

30

S	O	D	A		R	A	M	P	S		O	U	R	
T	K	O	S		E	X	I	L	E		U	T	E	S
E	R	G	S		V	E	N	O	M		T	A	N	S
P	A	C		M	I	L	K	P	I	T	C	H	E	R
			A	L	A	S			N	O	R			
O	C	T	A	N	E	S		C	O	P	Y	C	A	T
H	A	C	K	S		T	O	O	L	S		A	G	O
A	S	H	E		W	E	A	V	E		O	K	A	Y
R	T	E		T	H	E	R	E		C	R	E	P	E
A	E	R	O	S	O	L		S	N	U	B	B	E	D
			L	A	D			U	R	S	A			
S	L	E	D	R	U	N	N	E	R	S		T	N	T
H	O	W	E		N	E	E	D	S		S	T	E	W
E	V	E	S		I	M	A	G	E		D	E	C	O
E	S	T			T	O	T	E	D		I	R	K	S

31

D	R	O	P		E	N	C	L		B	A	B	E	L
R	E	P	O		D	A	L	I		I	N	L	A	Y
A	R	A	P		S	O	U	L		S	T	U	R	M
P	U	R	P	L	E	H	E	A	R	T		E	S	E
E	N	T	A	I	L			S	C	A	R	A	B	
			M	S	T		D	O	L	L	O	P		
O	R	G	A	N		H	O	R	A		I	O	N	A
C	O	R	D		S	E	W	E	R		B	O	E	R
H	U	E	D		L	E	N	D		D	I	D	I	T
			S	T	E	L	L	A		O	R	R		
	N	E	A	T	A	S		O	U	T	I	E	S	
F	A	B		Y	E	L	L	O	W	B	E	L	L	Y
O	R	A	T	E		S	A	V	E		N	E	I	N
R	I	C	E	R		O	V	E	R		O	N	T	O
T	A	K	E	S		P	E	N	S		N	E	E	D

32

	P	T	A		M	E	S	A		P	A	S		
A	L	A	S		A	R	A	L		A	T	A	L	L
B	O	X	S	P	R	I	N	G		R	O	X	I	E
E	D	I	T	I	O	N		A	M	A	Z	O	N	S
			S	L	O		L	E	A	D		P	A	T
B	A	N		O	N	T	O		N	O	S	H		
A	L	I	S	T		O	B	N	O	X	I	O	U	S
S	E	X	Y		O	R	S	O	N		A	N	T	E
E	X	O	N	E	R	A	T	E		S	M	E	A	R
			E	V	A		E	L	M	O		S	H	A
A	T	T		I	T	E	R		O	T	T			
C	H	A	N	C	E	L		A	T	T	R	A	C	T
T	O	P	O	T		F	O	X	H	O	U	N	D	S
I	R	E	N	E		I	D	L	E			C	O	R	E
S	O	D		N	E	E	R			E	N	S		

33

```
A P S O   B A H     U P D O S
R O C S   U N A   A R R I V E
C O R P O R A T E R A I D E R
S H A R K R E P E L L E N T
    P E A   R I L E     S O T
C O P Y   J O N     N E T
H O I     B O B S     A S T R O
E L L   E Y E   C P R   H O G
W A Y W E     L I E N     E A R
    E S P   I M P   F A D E
A P E     E M M A   S O U
  T A K E O V E R T A R G E T
G O L D E N P A R A C H U T E
O L E A R Y   D O N   E S T A
P L O Y S   E N G   S T A R
```

34

```
P I E R     A F I R E     M I E N
I N R E     R I D E S     I N D O
T E N D E R F O O T     S C I S
A R I E L     E L S A   T H E Y
T E A S E R       T H A W
      L E E     S E E K O U T
R A M S   R E A L   M E R R Y
A L I   H O T R O D S   M A P
S A L S A   T A P E   I S L E
P R E M I S E       A N N
    S A L T     E R A S E S
A C T S   A L A N   P I L E D
P O O H   Y A R D M A S T E R
S A N E   E L A T E   T O T E
O L E S   D A M O N   S N O W
```

35

```
B I G M A C     A R G O N A U T
A S T U T E     W A R H O R S E
T H O M A S D E Q U I N C E Y
        S T A R   U N O
D O T   R O G E T     C U F F
U N H I P   W O L   M I N O R
D O W N E A S T     S U N D R Y
    A N N I E O A K L E Y
E R R A N D     P S A L M I S T
B E T T Y   S O S   S A N T A
B A S E   H E T U P     G Y P
    F A R   C O O T
E L I Z A B E T H A S H L E Y
S O N A T I N A     C L E A V E
T U N G S T E N     H O Y D E N
```

36

```
C O S T   O V O I D   A S T A
A R I A   F O R N O   N C O S
P I T C H F O R K S   G R O W
T O A T E E   S A T I A T E
S N R   R R S     D E E P
    C A S T I R O N   B E D
T O T A L   U T E S   S O L E
A W O R D   P A N   A W O K E
L E S S   C O L E   B A K E R
E D S   T H R O W R U G
S A R A   S I S   A P E
B L A T A N T   S E R V E S
L A L O   C H U C K R O A S T
E V A N   E E R I E   M I T E
W A D E   S N E A D   E L S E
```

37

```
W A I T   M B E   G R A S S
A N N E   A R T S   R I N S E
L Y R E   C U T E   I N D E X
L O O N E Y T U N E S
O N A   L S U   T A T T L E S
W E D G E   S L O T   E A R S
      A N A   I F E   E N D S
L U N A T I C F R I N G E
S Y N D   O R K   Y R S
O N D E   N E S S   E Y E T O
U X O R I A L   C A N   Q E D
    C L A I R D E L U N E
J A B B A   N C A A   E A S T
A L I E N   D E P P   S T E T
B E G E T   S E T   S E R A
```

38

```
I D O L   H A R P     I T T O
N A P E   A G E E   A M O U R
I N A S   L I M E   R I N G S
T E L L I T L I K E I T I S
      I N S E T   R E A
P I P E T     S A L T I E R
A M I   R A T I O S   E L L A
T A L K O N E S H E A D O F F
E G A N   G A T O R S   N I T
R E F I L L S     K E A N S
    T E E   S T E E D
U T T E R A K I N D W O R D
I N R E D   M I L D   A B I E
S T A R S   O L D E   R E S T
M O M S   S L E D   D Y E S
```

39

```
S T A R   E S A U   U N F I T
U R S A   M A N S   P E O N Y
P O I N T O F N O R E T U R N
S T A T U T E S   E N T R E E
    I E R   N O D E
P I V O T S   T A P   D A M S
O R I B I   A R C E D   B A T
P E R I O D F U R N I T U R E
I N N   N O I S E   S A T I E
N E A T   C R T   M O R S E L
    E P E E   D U B
U N S E E N   D I S E A S E S
D O T M A T R I X S Y S T E M
O R I E L   E R I E   P E R U
S A R D S   V E E S   S M O G
```

40

```
C L A D   L A M B   H O S T S
H I D E   U V E A   O L L I E
A T O P   C O S T   G E E N A
T H R O W I N T H E T O W E L
S E N S E       A S T I
      E L M S   A E R I A L
E G O   D I E T S   A L F A
W A V E S A W H I T E F L A G
E G A N   S O L I D   S R S
S E L E C T     O M I T
      H I S S   T R A I T
H O L D U P O N E S H A N D S
A B O U T   N I L E   V I L A
R I N S E   A P S E   I T E R
M E E T S   R E E K   S A S S
```

41

```
C R A M   A L D A   S H A D E
H E R O   S E E S   E A S E L
A M O N T H O F S U N D A Y S
T I M E R       T E R I
S T A T U E S   T A L E N T S
      S M I T E   L E N O R E
W A S   A R A B S   I R A N
A L L O N E S B O R N D A Y S
V E I N   H E L I O   S S E
E R E C T S   D O L T S
      N A I L   F R E R E
F O R D O N K E Y S Y E A R S
A R B O R   H I E S   E R I E
R E I N S   S A W S   S E S S
```

42

```
S O L E   D E B I   S A T A N
A K I N   O L A N   E M I L E
M A S T   N A S A   R E E S E
B Y T R I A L A N D E R R O R
A S S E N T   L E A N
      T E C   D E S T R Y
A L T E R   L O A D   A R I A
B Y H O O K O R B Y C R O O K
E R I N   E T A L   R A N T S
T E N S O R   E W E
    C R A G   A D E S T E
O N E W A Y O R A N O T H E R
W A G E S   R O O T   H A N A
A M I L E   T U N E   E K E S
R U S T Y   A P E D   R O T E
```

43

```
J A M B   M A D A M   C O M B
A R I A   A L I C E   O P A L
B E E T   L I S T S   B I L E
A N T S I N H I S P A N T S
    L A C E     I L L E S T
D E R I D E   G R E A T
A R O N   C R U S T   M P S
F R O G I N H I S T H R O A T
T S K   N O O N E   E T T A
    A F R O S   D A S H E R
I N A R U T     A R N O
B E E I N H I S B O N N E T
E G O S   E D W I N   A X I S
A R N E   R E A D E   T E N T
M I S S   N A M E S   E D G Y
```

44

```
C A L M   S T E E D   P R O P
A G A R   W O L F E   R O P E
B R U S S E L S S P R O U T S
S A D   H A L E   L O W E S T
    C R T S   T E L L
T A U R U S   D A T E   A P R
A R S O N   B A K E   O B O E
B L A C K F O R E S T C A K E
L E G S   A R E S   R A T E D
E S E   A M E S   R U L E R S
    S L I D   P U M A
A G R E E S   A L M A   L A S
F R E N C H O N I O N S O U P
R I N D   E N T E R   A N N A
O D D S   D E E D S   P E T S
```

45

H	A	I	F	A		A	D	A	M		G	A	R	P
A	G	L	O	W		L	I	L	I		A	P	A	R
F	A	I	R	E		P	R	O	D		M	A	C	E
T	R	E	B	L	E		T	O	P	I	E	C	E	S
			R	E	S	T		F	O	S	T	E	R	S
R	H	E	O	S	T	A	T		I	L	E			
T	A	L	K	S		B	O	R	N	E		K	K	K
E	R	L	E		T	O	P	O	T		W	I	N	E
S	P	A		S	W	O	O	P		S	H	E	E	R
			B	E	E		L	E	F	T	O	V	E	R
A	W	A	I	T	E	D		D	I	A	L			
T	O	B	L	A	Z	E	S		B	R	E	A	D	S
S	O	I	L		E	V	I	L		T	H	R	O	E
E	D	D	Y		R	I	D	E		L	O	U	S	E
A	Y	E	S		S	L	E	D		E	G	G	E	D

46

C	O	K	E		R	A	N	G	E		S	L	A	T
O	D	I	N		I	D	O	L	S		T	A	R	O
M	O	L	D		C	O	L	E	P	O	R	T	E	R
A	R	L	E	N	E		A	N	C	I	E	N	T	
			E	M	U		F	I	N		E	T	N	A	S
E	M	B	I	T	T	E	R		T	L	C			
M	A	R	C		R	N	A		R	O	H	M	E	R
I	K	E		B	U	S	T	O	U	T		E	L	I
T	O	W	E	R	S		E	R	N		A	Y	I	N
			L	I	T		L	A	K	E	M	E	A	D
R	O	P	E	D		A	Y	N		A	I	R		
I	C	E	C	A	P	S		S	T	A	B	L	E	
T	A	T	T	L	E	T	A	L	E		B	E	E	N
A	L	E	E		N	O	V	E	L		L	E	N	D
S	A	R	D		T	R	A	I	L		E	R	A	S

47

A	B	A	S	E		W	I	T		F	A	S	T	S
R	A	C	E	R		I	D	O		U	T	T	E	R
A	L	L	I	E		N	E	W		N	O	R	A	S
B	L	A	Z	I	N	G	S	A	D	D	L	E	S	
L	O	S	E		A	S	T	R	O		L	A	P	S
E	T	S		P	O	P		D	E	L		M	O	I
			M	A	M	A	S			O	D	E	O	N
T	O	W	E	R	I	N	G	I	N	F	E	R	N	O
O	V	A	L	S			T	N	O	T	E			
G	E	T		E	M	S		D	T	S		E	T	O
A	R	C	H		C	L	A	U	S		A	L	I	D
C	H	A	R	I	O	T	S	O	F	F	I	R	E	
R	A	M	B	O		W	E	T		I	O	T	A	S
E	M	A	I	L		E	A	R		C	O	E	D	S
D	E	N	T	E		D	R	Y		A	T	S	E	A

48

C	L	A	M	P		D	R	O	P		S	O	D	A
P	A	L	E	R		R	A	G	E		A	L	A	N
O	B	E	S	E		O	M	E	N		D	E	N	T
	S	C	A	L	L	O	P	E	D	E	D	G	E	
			A	I	L	S		A	L	L				
S	H	A	S	T	A		K	N	E	E	C	A	P	
O	Y	S	T	E	R	W	H	I	T	E		E	V	A
N	E	T	S			H	E	N			A	D	E	N
I	N	A		C	L	A	M	D	I	G	G	E	R	S
C	A	R	S	E	A	T		T	O	A	S	T	Y	
			A	N	N		T	A	C	T				
	L	O	B	S	T	E	R	S	H	I	F	T	S	
L	O	R	E		E	R	I	K		N	E	A	L	S
E	V	E	R		R	I	P	E		T	A	R	O	T
T	E	S	S		N	E	E	D		O	R	A	T	E

49

P	A	P		S	O	S	O		J	U	I	C	E	
A	N	A		E	T	N	A		A	R	B	O	R	
L	Y	R	E		E	R	I	K		M	I	A	M	I
M	A	R	L	A	M	A	P	L	E	S		R	O	N
			M	I	L			S	A	R	I			
M	O	S	T	L	Y		N	O	N	C	O	M	S	
O	H	A	R	E		P	O	D	S		E	M	I	L
D	A	T	E	D		O	L	A		A	D	A	N	O
E	R	I	E		A	N	D	S		L	A	N	C	E
M	A	N	S	A	R	D			D	O	R	I	E	S
			B	A	E	R		R	N	S				
O	O	P		S	P	R	U	C	E	G	O	O	S	E
K	N	I	F	E		O	N	U	S		F	L	E	A
L	E	N	I	N		S	I	R	S		L	A	C	
A	L	E	R	T		A	N	D	Y		A	S	H	

50

B	A	R	R		S	A	B	R	A		A	D	Z	E
O	P	I	E		A	I	L	E	D		S	E	E	M
L	E	N	N	Y	B	R	U	C	E		P	A	S	T
O	R	D	E	A	L		R	E	P	R	I	N	T	S
			G	R	E	W		S	T	O	R	M		
S	I	R	E	N		A	S	S		M	E	A	R	A
T	S	A	R		F	R	I		M	A	D	R	I	D
A	L	Y		H	A	N	G	M	A	N		T	A	M
R	E	C	K	O	N		H	O	P		S	I	T	E
E	T	H	E	R		C	S	A		H	U	N	A	N
			A	N	N	U	L		B	L	O	C		
C	O	R	N	E	R	E	D		I	N	C	H	E	S
A	B	L	E		B	R	I	A	N	K	E	I	T	H
N	O	E	L		A	G	A	P	E		E	R	N	E
T	E	S	S		N	Y	L	O	N		D	E	A	D

51

M	A	A	M	S		B	A	B	O		O	A	F	S
A	G	G	I	E		R	E	A	M		A	R	I	A
C	H	I	N	E	S	E	C	H	E	C	K	E	R	S
S	A	N	D	M	A	N		T	R	A	I	N	E	E
			E	T	T	A		T	R	E	A	D	S	
L	A	R	E	D	O		S	A	A	R				
A	G	A	R		N	A	C	L		E	L	I	A	S
R	U	S	S	I	A	N	R	O	U	L	E	T	T	E
D	E	P	T	S		T	I	E	R		N	O	M	E
			T	R	I	B		A	T	O	N	E	D	
S	A	R	T	R	E		E	T	N	A				
T	S	A	R	I	N	A		E	U	R	A	S	I	A
I	N	D	I	A	N	W	R	E	S	T	L	I	N	G
L	E	A	P		I	R	A	N		A	P	A	C	E
E	R	R	S		E	Y	E	S		N	O	M	A	D

52

A	R	C		R	A	I	D	S		A	D	E	S	
B	A	R	B		A	P	R	O	N		B	A	B	A
O	V	E	R		F	E	E	T	O	F	C	L	A	Y
M	E	D	E	A		N	E	R	O		I	N	S	
B	L	O	W	S	O	N	E	S	T	O	P			
			S	I	R	E			S	T	R	A	P	S
C	H	A		A	S	S	E	S		O	L	I	O	
H	A	V	E	N	O	T	R	U	C	K	W	I	T	H
I	D	E	A		S	A	L	O	N			T	H	O
P	A	R	R	O	T			F	L	E	E			
			P	L	A	Y	B	A	L	L	W	I	T	H
E	P	A		A	M	O	R			T	E	R	R	A
G	O	F	L	Y	A	K	I	T	E		R	A	I	N
G	O	R	E		L	E	N	I	N		S	T	L	O
S	L	O	G		E	D	G	E	D		E	L	I	

53

A	G	H	A	S	T		A	D	A		L	E	A	
S	H	R	I	N	E	R		D	I	X		I	N	C
W	O	O	D	Y	W	O	O	D	P	E	C	K	E	R
A	L	C		A	U	T	H			A	E	R	O	
N	E	E	R		P	H	O	E	B	E	S	N	O	W
			R	A	P			T	O	N	E			
A	R	I	S	E		G	O	N	N	A		D	E	E
T	H	E	P	E	L	I	C	A	N	B	R	I	E	F
E	O	S		W	R	I	T	S			L	A	R	K	S
			A	E	O	N				E	S	T		
T	H	E	P	E	N	G	U	I	N		A	B	C	S
A	O	N	E			S	N	O	B			I	R	E
S	A	N	D	I	E	G	O	C	H	I	C	K	E	N
T	R	I		L	Y	E		A	I	R	I	E	S	T
E	D	S		L	E	M		S	T	R	E	S	S	

54

H	A	H	A		A	M	E	N		H	A	D	I	T
O	V	E	N		R	A	V	E		O	L	I	V	E
S	A	L	T		T	H	E	B	L	U	E	M	A	X
T	I	L	L		S	A	N		A	S	S	E	N	T
S	L	O	E	S		L	I	S	L	E				
		D	R	O	P		N	E	O		A	B	E	T
S	R	O		R	O	U	G	E		S	H	U	L	A
D	O	L	O	R	E	S		P	O	M	A	D	E	S
A	L	L	A	Y		I	S	S	U	E		D	E	S
K	E	Y	S		N	N	E		R	A	C	Y		
			P	A	G	E	S		R	A	B	A	T	
E	L	D	E	R	S		S	A	M		M	U	C	H
D	I	R	T	Y	H	A	R	R	Y		E	D	I	E
I	R	A	T	E		T	E	A	R		O	D	D	S
T	A	T	E	R		E	D	N	A		N	Y	S	E

55

A	R	I	A		S	A	B	L	E	S		A	H	A
P	E	N	D		T	R	O	L	L	S		N	O	B
H	P	L	O	V	E	C	R	A	F	T		N	A	B
I	L	O		E	P	S	O	M		S	E	X	Y	
D	O	V	I	S	H		A	C	T	O	R			
S	W	E	E	T	E	S	T		L	I	M	I	T	S
			R	A	N	D	Y		I	C	E	C	A	P
M	A	J		K	I	R	O	V			E	R	A	
A	D	O	N	A	I		O	N	E	G	A			
D	E	H	O	R	N		S	I	B	I	L	A	N	T
			N	U	D	G	E		A	Z	A	L	E	A
B	O	S	N		R	E	A	R	M			O	A	R
I	R	A		D	E	A	N	R	K	O	O	N	T	Z
T	A	U		A	R	S	I	N	E		A	S	E	A
E	L	L		S	E	E	D	E	R		T	O	R	N

56

S	L	E	W		B	A	M	B	I		S	P	A	T
I	O	T	A		A	R	I	A	S		P	A	B	A
M	A	U	I		R	I	N	S	E		A	R	O	N
P	N	I	N		R	E	D	H	E	R	R	I	N	G
			S	H	E	L			E	S	S	E	S	
B	E	A	C	O	N		S	K	A	T	E			
A	C	T	O	N		J	A	I	L			L	O	U
W	H	I	T	E	C	O	L	L	A	R	J	O	B	S
L	O	T			O	M	E	N		A	E	G	I	S
			M	S	D	O	S		V	E	T	O	E	R
A	B	B	E	Y			R	E	S	T				
B	L	U	E	R	I	B	B	O	N		I	F	F	Y
Y	O	R	K		P	E	A	S	E		S	I	R	E
S	A	K	E		S	A	T	I	E		O	V	E	N
S	T	E	R		O	T	H	E	R		N	E	T	S

57
```
LIV KOOP SPAHN
ROLE NOVA PAREE
IDOL ONEI INTRO
BENCHWARRANT
SARAH ASIA SLO
ONOR MCBAIN
MAD SWINGSHIFTS
ASIS LOU GERE
CHAIRPERSON SET
RENNIE TSAR
ORE OSLO SNEAK
STOOLPIGEONS
SPATE ODIC KRIS
ASTOR SELL ETTA
WIMPS ERLE DAS
```

58
```
ATTAR GALA LODE
SAUTE ABED ANEW
KILOS ZUIDERZEE
INANE ELDERS
IMPALA AGRA
CABLED BESTOWED
EMU SETON RODE
ABLE RILES BOWL
GOBY BITES DAT
ESSENCES RIVERA
OATH GRINDS
STAIRS DELES
WINDMILLS ONHER
IDOL NEMO INONE
GENE OWNS NEEDY
```

59
```
PITCH MCAN EVAN
ATRIA ARNO LIDO
THECYCLONE ETON
HEXA OTO LAVABO
DANANG SALES
MCCANN REST
PRO TEPEES OER
HURRICANECARTER
ZEE TICTAC AAA
USSR PESTLE
STONE SAGEST
TONITE LEE ANDI
EXIT GALESAYERS
NICE GMAN ROREM
ONES SANA SNOWY
```

60
```
APSE LIZA AFLAT
BONN IRIS NIECE
BLACKBOOK TRAIN
ALGAE NNE WENDS
MST WHET
TRAPEZES ERRATA
HIS YELLOWPAGES
ACTS SAM PRAY
WHITEPAPERS ERE
SERAPE SNAKIEST
LIAR DIN
BAWLS AAS MAMAS
ACHOO BLUEPRINT
EMEND ISPY OTTO
RENEE DOSE WEEP
```

61
```
SHAPE FALA ARAB
PUTON EGAN SELA
ALONG NEON SCAN
TAPDANCESAROUND
GOES ARRAY
FEEDERS GRIT
ABLE SOOT OAT
TAKESTWOTOTANGO
ENE OVAL ICES
RYAN AIMLESS
ADIEU ALSO
WALTZINGTHROUGH
ALOT DARE ATRIA
RENO OVER START
DYAN LEES SOLOS
```

62
```
BLAB SCOFF JOB
RULE HAGAR TOBE
ANON ALLIE REIN
SCHINDLERSLIST
SHANE SCAM
GENUS OBTUSE
PSS URAL EASED
STEVENSPIELBERG
SAGET APSE DEE
TRASHY YALTA
PIES ARSON
THECOLORPURPLE
HAIR MOVER ERSE
AXES AMINE SEED
MID NODES TENS
```

63
```
SIAM MAC FELL
ISLE VICES AREA
THISLITTLEPIGGY
MON ALTAR
TALENT SOUR GPS
OCARINA PICARO
LEVI ELLS ALDEN
RAZORBACKHOGS
ABLER AGAR DEAN
NISSAN RIGHTLY
ACE COMB NOOSES
ALBEE GNP
THREELITTLEPIGS
HAIR ENSUE EVEL
ELMO EYE RELY
```

64
```
BOSH TBAR GOBI
ERTE RENO HEMAN
ANEW ODAY AMENS
DOWNHILLSKIING
STS AKA URN
MIAMIINDIANS
ENROL TOTO LIL
GOAD HANNA SANE
ARM PALO RESEW
NAPOLIITALIA
NET NAP TAI
HAWAIIANISLAND
LANAS ASAN ATNO
STORE NILE VEIL
TEND SASS ARES
```

65
```
LIMB SHIED DOKE
ASIA AINTI AMOS
ILLS STATS MICE
TELEPHONEBOOTH
MIEN URN
AGREES NORD FTC
BRAN MOOSE SRO
BIGTIMEOPERATOR
ONE RAINS DOTE
TDS OGRE TROPHY
ANN CHAR
THEYELLOWPAGES
GRAS TIARA BRIE
OUZO INNER LONE
BEEP COAST EWER
```

66
```
LOAF LADY ADAMS
ABBA EIRE BOWIE
NOEL ADOS SWALE
DELL NAP DUNKED
ODE STARTER
CRAVED OUTDO
HAVEN JUNE TBAR
ICER COTES HONE
NERO IDOS PEENS
NOTIF REGRET
TEEPEES EAR
BIASED ISM OAST
ALTER AGEE ULNA
ADELA SHAD NOON
SERFS ATRY DUBS
```

67
```
TIAS LURE ROBES
ANNE AREA EPEES
POKEFUNAT TELLS
ENAMOR SAINT
LESS PLEBES
COSTELLO RERULE
ANTSY ACHED CAW
SERE TIKIS SKYE
POI CANED FILER
ANKERS YEARNERS
REEVES ERLE
GAMES ESPRIT
RHODO PUNCHLINE
GALEN ERIK OLDE
SIDRA DEBS PEON
```

68
```
MAMA TIKES ADDS
ARID ANEST THUD
DASH RJREYNOLDS
DBCOOPER LANAS
CHOC SINEW
LBJ ANTENNA RED
ORDERS DIG LEGO
PASTE SGT TANGO
EVAS CUE SUCCOR
SOL CHEROOT ENS
ISLES ROTE
ANTED YATITTLE
BFGOODRICH HAIL
OREL APPLE ELLA
BORE RISES REIN
```

69

S	T	O	I	C		A	M	A		W	H	E	E	L
S	I	D	C	A	E	S	A	R		R	A	L	L	Y
S	T	E	A	M	B	O	A	T	W	I	L	L	I	E
			N	E	O	N	S			E	S	S		
M	C	S		R	A	G		J	E	T		C	T	R
O	R	T	H	A	T		C	O	P		T	R	I	O
Z	I	P	A	D	E	E	D	O	O	D	A	H		
S	I	D	E	N	O	T	E	S		M	E	T	O	O
R	E	E	D		G	E	L		F	E	D	O	R	A
I	R	S		D	D	S		S	A	W		R	N	S
		S	E	A		F	A	T	H	A				
M	I	C	K	E	Y	M	O	U	S	E	C	L	U	B
A	C	R	I	D		E	X	C	O	R	I	A	T	E
P	E	O	N	S		W	Y	E		E	D	G	E	D

70

S	M	A	R	T		A	D	M	A	N		B	E	T
A	C	T	O	R		B	O	I	S	E		U	T	E
B	I	L	L	Y	T	H	E	K	I	D		F	H	A
		A	S	H	O	R	E			A	F	A	R	
C	H	A	N	T	E	R	S		P	A	G	A	N	S
H	A	N	D				L	A	P	E	L			
U	R	N		N	E	L	S	O	N	S		O	L	D
T	R	I		O	V	E	R	L	I	E		B	E	E
E	Y	E		M	A	N	I	A	C	S		I	V	E
			O	M	E	N	S				S	L	E	D
L	E	A	R	N	S		A	P	O	S	T	L	E	S
A	R	K	S			G	R	A	D	E	A			
C	A	L		C	O	L	E	Y	O	U	N	G	E	R
E	S	E		A	L	O	N	E		S	C	A	R	Y
D	E	Y		D	E	B	A	R		S	E	D	G	E

71

A	L	T	O	S		M	E	R	C		P	H	E	W
F	E	I	N	T		B	L	A	H		L	A	T	E
R	A	D	I	I		A	B	I	E		A	N	T	A
O	N	E	O	F	A		O	L	E	A	N	D	E	R
			I	N	F	L	O	W			R	D	A	
B	U	S	Y		L	A	S		L	A	R	Y	N	X
I	S	H		T	S	K		B	E	G		E	E	R
D	E	I		A	Y	E		L	A	I		S	R	A
E	R	G		U	S	N		A	D	O		I	V	Y
T	S	H	I	R	T		O	R	E		A	M	Y	S
		S	U	E		B	E	R	B	E	R			
T	R	A	N	S	M	I	T		S	U	R	E	S	T
W	A	N	T		S	N	A	P		L	I	A	N	E
O	M	N	I		G	A	I	L		L	A	D	E	R
S	P	O	T		O	N	N	O		S	L	Y	E	R

72

B	A	B	A	S		K	A	L	E		A	F	A	R
E	L	A	T	E		I	R	O	N		L	A	R	A
E	L	S	E	S		T	A	T	A		S	W	I	M
P	A	S	S	T	H	E	B	U	C	K		N	A	P
	T	O	T	E	A		S	T	E	N	S			
			S	T	I	N	G		S	E	N	O	R	A
A	C	E		F	A	R	R		N	E	V	E	R	
H	A	L		V	A	M	O	O	S	E		E	D	T
A	N	K	L	E		E	A	S	E		R	O	Y	
B	E	H	E	S	T		N	A	N	C	E			
	O	A	T	E	R		T	A	S	K	S			
S	T	U		S	T	A	G	P	A	R	T	I	E	S
T	U	N	A		O	N	E	O		H	A	N	D	Y
E	N	D	S		N	E	R	D		O	T	T	E	R
M	E	S	H		S	E	E	S		P	E	E	R	S

73

R	A	M	P		E	M	M	A	S		U	S	E	D
I	D	E	A		M	E	D	I	A		S	T	A	Y
B	O	W	D	L	E	R	I	S	M		H	A	V	E
			O	R	E		L	O	W	E	R	E	D	
	A	P	I	N	G		R	E	V	E	R	B		
A	V	O	N		E	V	E		A	S	S	O	R	T
T	E	R	R		D	E	P	O	R	T		A	I	R
E	N	T	E	R		E	L	K		S	E	R	V	E
A	G	E		E	A	S	I	E	R		I	D	E	S
M	E	R	G	E	S		E	Y	E		N	E	T	S
		H	O	S	T	E	D		L	E	E	R	S	
	L	O	O	T	E	R	S		C	A	L			
A	B	U	T		I	S	A	A	C	S	T	E	R	N
R	O	S	E		D	E	N	S	E		A	R	E	A
K	E	E	N		E	N	D	E	D		B	A	B	Y

74

A	B	R	A			I	S	T			S	H	A	M
I	D	L	E	S		A	N	T	I		E	E	R	O
M	O	U	T	H	O	R	G	A	N		T	A	N	S
A	R	E	A		S	T	A	R	C	H		D	O	T
S	E	R	I	E	S			S	T	I	L	L		
			L	A	I	N	E		S	P	O	I	L	
R	A	F		R	E	E	D	S		J	A	N	E	T
A	D	A	I	R		A	G	A		O	M	E	G	A
M	M	C	D	I		L	A	N	D	I		S	O	X
	S	E	E	N	O		R	E	I	N	S			
	V	A	G	U	E			A	T	O	N	A	L	
A	R	A		S	T	R	A	I	N		F	A	L	A
T	I	L	E		F	I	N	G	E	R	T	I	P	S
O	P	U	S		O	C	T	O		F	I	V	E	S
P	E	E	P		R	A	E		K	E	E	N		

75

S	H	A	G		H	A	G	A	R		G	L	O	P
G	A	L	E		O	M	E	G	A		R	E	N	O
T	H	E	T	H	R	E	E	S	T	O	O	G	E	S
			Z	O	N	E	S			I	O	O		
C	S	A		M	E	R		T	O	P	M	O	S	T
C	E	N	T	E	R		S	O	N	S		U	T	E
S	A	D	I	E		T	I	N	A		E	T	A	L
	M	O	E	C	U	R	L	Y	L	A	R	R	Y	
G	I	R	D		N	E	T	S		T	O	A	S	T
O	E	R		O	D	E	S		F	E	S	C	U	E
T	R	A	P	P	E	D		A	R	M		E	P	A
			O	U	R		I	N	A	P	T			
S	L	A	P	S	T	I	C	K	C	O	M	E	D	Y
S	A	R	I		O	C	A	L	A		E	R	I	E
T	W	I	N		W	I	N	E	S		N	A	G	S

76

M	A	L	T		W	A	I	S	T		C	H	O	P
I	L	I	E		O	R	D	I	E		D	E	M	O
S	T	E	R	E	O	T	Y	P	E		C	A	A	N
C	O	N	R	A	D		L	A	T	H		D	R	Y
			O	S	L	O		T	E	E	U	P		
M	I	S	R	E	A	D	S		R	A	S	H	E	R
A	M	I		S	N	O	W		L	E	O	N	A	
C	E	N	T		D	R	I	L	L		S	N	U	G
	H	A	G	A	R		P	I	E	S		E	R	E
E	N	L	I	S	T		E	N	T	H	U	S	E	D
	E	L	V	E	S			O	D	I	N			
R	E	F		P	A	C	S		O	R	D	E	R	S
A	X	I	S		C	O	P	Y	W	R	I	T	E	R
M	A	L	E		U	N	I	O	N		E	T	A	T
A	M	E	N		P	E	N	N	S		S	U	R	A

77

B	I	O		R	I	F	F			A	M	M	O	
E	R	N	S		O	N	A	I	R		R	E	A	R
N	A	S	A		S	H	U	S	H		E	R	R	S
T	H	E	G	R	E	E	N	H	O	R	N	E	T	
E	M	C	E	E		R	A	H		N	A	D	I	A
R	A	T		H	O	E		O	H	S		I	N	N
			T	A	G		Z	O	O		S	T	E	T
	T	H	E	B	L	U	E	K	N	I	G	H	T	
C	R	U	X		E	N	D		O	C	T			
D	E	L		M	S	T		O	R	I		A	M	I
S	E	A	L	S		I	A	N		N	A	B	O	B
	T	H	E	G	O	L	D	E	N	G	I	R	L	S
P	O	O	F		I	N	D	I	A		K	A	T	E
S	P	O	T		L	O	L	L	S		E	D	E	N
I	S	P	Y		W	E	L	T		N	E	D		

78

S	E	A	T		U	R	S	A		B	E	T	A	S
A	X	L	E		S	E	A	M		A	T	O	N	E
G	A	L	E	S	O	F	L	A	U	G	H	T	E	R
S	C	A	P	E		A	S	P			E	A	T	
	T	H	E	W	I	N	D	S	O	F	W	A	R	
		E	S	T	E			N	A	H				
S	P	A		I	R	I	S		R	E	P	O	S	
H	A	I	L	A	N	D	F	A	R	E	W	E	L	L
	A	L	L	A	Y		S	A	B	U		T	E	Y
			N	A	E		I	N	T	O				
	L	I	G	H	T	N	I	N	G	B	U	G	S	
P	E	R		C	O	N		A	T	R	E	E		
F	O	R	D	T	H	U	N	D	E	R	B	I	R	D
C	R	E	D	O		N	E	O	N		I	M	A	N
S	A	G	E	T		S	R	T	A		D	E	L	A

79

T	I	E	R		D	E	I	S	M		S	L	A	B
O	N	M	E		O	L	D	I	E		P	O	L	E
W	H	I	T	E	Y	F	O	R	D		L	U	T	E
N	O	L	O	V	E		L	E	I		I	G	O	R
S	T	E	W	I	N	G		A	O	N	E			
			E	L	S	I	E		T	E	T	H	E	R
B	O	Y	D	S		V	A	D	E	R		R	A	T
E	L	O		M	E	S	A	S		I	V	E		
G	G		S	A	N	E	R		L	U	G	E	S	
T	A	I	L	O	R		S	E	T	I	N			
	B	A	L	I			D	O	L	L	A	R	S	
A	M	E	N		M	F	A		P	L	A	N	E	T
H	A	R	D		B	I	L	L	D	I	C	K	E	Y
A	C	R	E		A	L	A	M	O		E	L	S	E
B	E	A	D		S	L	I	N	G		D	E	E	S

80

P	A	S	T		G	I	L	A		N	O	S	E	S
O	W	A	R		A	D	A	M		E	T	H	A	N
S	A	D	A		B	O	L	A		A	T	A	R	I
T	R	A	I	L	B	L	A	Z	E	R		D	S	T
S	E	T	T	E	E			E	N	E	R	O		
			O	R	S	O		T	R	A	W	L	S	
S	A	T	O	N		P	I	E	R		I	B	I	S
E	G	A	D		M	A	L	L	E		S	O	R	T
R	E	I	D		I	T	E	M		S	E	X	E	S
	A	R	L	E	N	S		D	O	N	A			
	G	R	E	E	T			A	M	A	N	D	A	
A	B	A		T	R	A	C	K	R	E	C	O	R	D
P	E	T	I	T		C	H	A	R		T	R	E	E
S	T	E	V	E		K	E	N	O		O	V	A	L
E	A	S	E	D		S	T	E	W		R	O	M	E

81

```
M O A T   F U R     P R I D E
A H S O   O L A F   R I C E D
J A C K S O N F I V E S O N G
A R I E T T A   D E T E N T E
S E I N E R   W O R E
      T E L E   A N G L E R
E S S O   S O L O   S L I C E
S L A P S T I C K W E A P O N
T I B E T   N O R A   D O N E
A M U L E T   M A L T
      I O N E   L E G M A N
A R R A N G E   R E A L I Z E
S O F T W A R E B Y L O T U S
H Y D R A   F O I E   B E S T
E S S A Y   S S S   S R A S
```

82

```
E T A L   I N D I A   S L A B
L A N A   N E O N S   P A V E
A R T S   B R I G H T I D E A
M A E S T R O   I N E R T
      O W E   T O T E D
S A G E A D V I C E   L A D A
A D O R N   I M E T   E L E M
C A R   G A V E L E D   O V I
K N E W   P A S O   R U N I N
S O D A   A C U T E A N G L E
S T R E P   N F L
T A S T E   A Z T E C A N
S M A R T M O N E Y   A L M A
A M I E   A L A R M   S U P S
R O L L   C A N O E   H E S A
```

83

```
A L B U M   B R A C   G E D
B O O N E   L I M O   A R A B
B A T E S   A S I N   Z I N A
E M T   S I D E E F F E C T S
      O C H R E   L A T H E S
P A M P A S   T W I X T
S I S A L   C H I C   E B B S
S T U   L O Y A L T Y   A R E
T S P S   R A N T   O P C I T
      C L I N K   T R I K E S
O C T A V E   C A K E D
D O W N I N F R O N T   R O M
E N I D   T A I L   O M A N I
S E T A   E R T E   W A F E R
Y S L   D O E S   N I T R O
```

84

```
C A M E   G U L C H   A F R O
A V I V   A P A R T   P L A T
N I N E   R U B E S   P O R T
C A T N A P P E D   C L U E
A T E S T   L O C O   N F L
N E D   L E S   R O A D I E
    S A L T I N E   M E E T
  E A T S L I K E A B I R D
A L M A   E R E C T E D
S K A T E R   K E N   B A R
S S R   L Y E S   N O O N E
  C E L L   L U C K Y D O G S
A L T O   H A D O N   O G L E
G U T S   S T A T E   R I O T
O B O E   T E N S E   S E S S
```

85

```
A S T A   A S I T   T W A S
G E E S   R U T H S   H E R E
U P T H E C R E E K   A L I E
A T H E N A   R E O I L E D
      S T R E A M I N   S L Y
D U D   R O L E   N E A P
E L O P E   E R A S   F R E D
A N N I E   N O S   D A I L Y
R A N K   C A S T   A R N I E
      Y E A R   O I N K   G A S
E B B   P O O L R O O M
C A R T O O N   O T I O S E
O B O E   K E E P S A T B A Y
L E O N   S I N C E   C I T E
E L K S   N E T S   H E E D
```

86

```
P A N G   A M B I T   A B B A
A P O D   M A L T A   R E U P
B E L A B A R T O K   M A R S
A S O N A N T   E M B R Y O
      S H A   A B A C A B
B U B K A   S L O   I N R E D
A S I   M A L A G A   D Y N A
C U L   A L I B A B A   A S U
K A L B   S C A R A B   N U B
S L Y A S   E M T   S A T E S
      B R E N D A   B O B
B R A N C A   B A R B I E S
L O R E   B A R R Y B O N D S
A T T Y   O L D I E   T S A R
B O Y S   B A S E R   T O M S
```

87

```
Y O Y O   A R E A L   C H E W
O D O R   B I A L Y   H A L O
R O U T   H A S O N   A M I R
E M S   P O N Y E X P R E S S
      E V E R T   E A G L E T
P A N E L S   D A Y N E
A N D R E   M O N E T   E L M
L A M B   P I N E D   A M I E
S T E   M A C A W   A R I S E
      T A S K S   S C U L P T
A B B O T T   P U T T Y
F O R W A R D P A S S   P S A
T R E E   A I R E S   L O O M
R E E L   M O O S E   I S L E
A D D S   I N D E X   E T O N
```

88

```
A B A B   S P R Y   S M I T H
B O N O   C L U E   T A H O E
U N T O   R U L A   R I A T A
S U I T C A S E S   E L D E R
E S C H E W   T R A P
      E L A N   S M O K E S
P A N G S   M I R V   U L N A
A L O U   H E T U P   C E O S
T E R N   O N E S   C H E W S
S C A N T Y   R E A L
      Y E T I   N A S S A U
C A U S E   B A C K P A C K S
U N C A P   S I L L   B O R E
D O L C E   E D I E   O N O R
S N A K E   N A P S   T E N S
```

89

```
S O D A S   B R A V O   S A L
A R E N A   R O M A N   P L U
G R A N D F I N A L E   E L M
      I D L E   S I T   C O P
A N G E L A   D I M I T Y
T A R   E M B E D   M I A
T O E   B A L I   E F L A T
I M A S   E L I A S   F I L E
C I T E D   L O N I   S I N
      D A R   S T A T S   T K O
S M I L E S   C H A S E R
T O V   S O S   P O O R
E L I   S U P E R M A R K E T
A D D   U S A G E   L A I N E
L Y E   P A N G S   S Y N G E
```

90

```
M E W L   R A I S A   D A D S
A C H E   E R R O R   O B I E
C H E A P T R I C K   R E A R
H O N D U R A S   F E L L A
R E N   Z O O M
    T R E A T W I L L I A M S
R O U T E D   H O E D   D A H
A N T E   B I N   N O R A
P E T   S I L L   S M E R S H
T R I C K Q U E S T I O N
      R I S E   P A D
B E B O P   S E S S I O N S
E V A S   D U T C H T R E A T
S E R B   B R A K E   M I N E
S L A Y   A B Y S S   A L A N
```

91

```
P H I L   A N K A   D E I F Y
R O N A   S E E M   E X T R A
I G E T   E X P O   B I S O N
C A P E H A T T E R A S
E N T R Y   B A T T L E S
      P A S S A G E   I L E
B O O T E D U P   S U E D E
A F R O   S M A S H   S T E M
R A I N S   T I E S C O R E
E G O   M A E S T R O
D E N S E L Y   L I M B O
    L A T E B L O O M E R S
C I G A R   L O O M   B R I C
A W A K E   I N C A   A L D A
M O P E D   D O O R   D E E R
```

92

```
A R A B   S L O W   A D M I T
R O U E   H A N A   T E A R Y
T A T A   A N O N   O T T E R
S M O K E S C R E E N   C N O
      E R T E   D A S H E S
N U T R I A   B E D L A M
A R O S E   D E L I   N A T O
S I R   S T E A M E D   K E N
A S C H   R E D S   I D E A L
H I R E R S   F A I R L Y
G U S T A V   A I N T
U S O   F I R E C R A C K E R
S A N I T   A L U M   H A R I
T I G R E   M E T E   E L A N
O R S E R   P E E R   D E S K
```

93

```
L A T H E   B A R R   C L E F
A R R A Y   O P I E   H A R E
S L I M E   L A N D   A I D E
T E C H   P O R K B A R R E L
S N E A K S     O P T
    N E I G H B O R   A S I
G L A D E   R O O K   G U T S
R I V E N   E R N   M O R A L
A M I D   V A S E   O H A R E
Y E S   W A T E R L O O
    P A C     E G G N O G
P I G I N A P O K E   W O R E
O N Y X   N O T A   F I T I N
E T R E   C L A Y   F L E E R
T O O L   Y O Y O   A D D L E
```

94

```
E M I T S   F R E T   A B C S
B E R R A   D E L E   E R L E
B R A I N D R A I N   R I A L
S E N D E R   M A E   O G R E
      E R O S   S T A S H E S
D A W N   O L E   S L O T
A L I T   P I M A   O L I V E
L A S   E Y E B R O W   D O E
I N E R T   R E I D   T E L L
    C E N T   R E D   E A T S
C E R T A I N   S E L A
O M A R   N I P   S A R A H S
M I C E   S M A R T M O N E Y
I L K A   E B R O   P O N E S
C E S T   L I E D   S M E L T
```

95

```
M A S S     R I T A   G N P
A D I E U   S U S H I   R I O
O S C A R W I N N E R   A N S
      B A N G O R   S C A T
T O G A S   S T E V I E
S I L E N T S     S A M P A N
A R I D   E A T S   N I E C E
L A V   I S L A N D S   R O E
A D E P T   E R I E   B I R D
D E B R I S   P A T R O N S
R A S H E S   R O A D S
S T A Y   E V I C T S
H U N   F A I T H H E A L E R
A B C   A R T I E   E M I L Y
H A H   A S A N   O P I E
```

96

```
P R O S   H I P P O   C H A R
A U N T   O D E O N   H A L O
P E C A N R O L L S   I M A M
A R E N A S   T I E C L A S P
    D I E S   S T E I N
A W F U L   A S H   R E D U B
H A R P   R I O   P E S E T A
A C E   R E D U C E S   G I N
B O S S E D   S U N   O G L E
H I P   P E R   F U S E S
A L F A L F A   B R U T
F A R M Y A R D   A R R O W S
T R U E   C O R N F L A K E S
E G I S   E D I C T   G R I T
R O T E   T Y P O S   E A R S
```

97

```
P A N S Y   R A C E R   A W L
A L I C E   A G O R A   C O E
P O L A R I C E C A P   C P O
S E E M   R I N K   S A R A N
    P L A N T A R   R A T E
A L L   U S E   T O U T
N E I L L   T O A D I E R
D E M O L I T I O N D E R B Y
R E V E R I E   E R N I E
E D I T   A P R   O S S
T A X I   S O U R E S T
O W E N S   I N G A   A E R O
P A N   C O S M O T O P P E R
P R O   A N T E S   P E E V E
S E N   T E S T Y   T R E S S
```

98

```
S P A R E   F L E D   S P O T
H A S A T   R A N I   T O G A
A R T I C H O K E S   E K E S
D E A L   O N E   A G R E E S
    W O R D   L E E R S
S A H A R A   H A L L O F
P L O Y S   H A L O   S A N G
A O K   O K I N A W A   C O L
S T E P   I N K S   G R E T A
Y E A S T S   S E E D E D
A P E R S   L I S T
G L O R I A   A I R   I R A S
R A K E   B A C K S T R O K E
A M E S   L I R E   R E S I N
B O Y S   E D E N   I D E N T
```

99

```
S A R A H   B U M P   M A D
S P I R A L   E S A U   O N E
R E V E R E   L A I R   A K A _
  S E N E G A L   N E C T A R
    R O M   L E S S E R
S O F T   U P S E T   A D U B
C A R   C P O   A R I Z O N A
A T O A S T     E V E N T S
L E N G T H S   R A Y   N I T
E S T A   E P S O M   L Y L E
    I N C A N T   S O B
C O R N E R   A I R P O R T
O R O   R E E K   P E K O E S
K A T   V E R E   I N T O T O
E L S   E K E D     T O K E N
```

100

```
B L E D   L O P E D   R E S T
A I D E   O R A T E   E R I E
C L I P   R A S T A   L I N D
H I T T H E R O A D J A C K
      O L E     S O X
S A B L E   T E E N   A M I
P L A Y I T A G A I N S A M
T I L L   H U G   O K R A
B E A M M E U P S C O T T Y
A S H   U R G E   O R E O S
    S N O   O N T
S A Y I T A I N T S O J O E
B O L L   I N D I E   P A B A
B L I P   C O L O N   U N I T
B O T H   A N E N T   S E T S
```